A DAY IN SPIRIT

A Spiritual Calendar for Teens

Dearest Chloe,

May you always walk in the light & be the precious light that you are with your Angels by your side.

In love & light,
Lilli Pattilo

Other Books by Nikki Pattillo

Children of the Stars

A Spiritual Evolution

A DAY IN SPIRIT

A Spiritual Calendar for Teens

Nikki Pattillo

Quinn Press

Asheville, North Carolina

Copyright @ 2016 Nikki Pattillo

All rights reserved. No part of this book may be reproduced or utilized in any form or by any means, electronic or mechanical, including photocopying, recording, or by any information storage and retrieval system, without permission in writing from the publisher.

Library of Congress Cataloging-in-Publication Data

Pattillo, Nikki, author.
   A day in spirit : a daily calendar for teens / by Nikki Pattillo.
   pages cm
   LCCN 2016931812
   ISBN 978-0-9911532-5-1

   1. New Age devotional calendars--Juvenile literature. 2. Teenagers--Prayers and devotions--Juvenile literature. 3. Devotional literature. 4. Prayers. [1. New Age devotional calendars. 2. Prayer books and devotions.]   I. Title.

BP605.N48P388 2016   299'.930835
                                QBI16-600030

Printed in the United States

Published by

QUINN PRESS

Asheville, North Carolina

To Maddy

You remind me every day that this world must change.

TABLE OF CONTENTS

ACKNOWLEDGMENTS xi

JANUARY 1

FEBRUARY 17

MARCH 31

APRIL 47

MAY 61

JUNE 77

JULY 91

AUGUST 107

SEPTEMBER 123

OCTOBER 137

NOVEMBER 153

DECEMBER 167

ACKNOWLEDGMENTS

Once again I find the need to thank my team. To my Angels and Guides who are so very patient with me when I find every excuse not to sit and write. Thank you for allowing me to help make this world a better place in any little way that I can. Thank you for being with me and for giving me messages of hope and inspiration to share with all that will walk a spiritual path.

Thank you to my daughter Maddy for being in my life. Your love and special energy gives me hope for our Earth and the people on it. I pray that through my path, I can make things easier for you in yours.

This calendar is dedicated to the thousands of people who have emailed me asking for help in their journeys. You have agreed to come to this Earth on a group mission as lightworkers to help living and non–living things because you are souls that are brave enough and strong enough to do this. Never forget who you are and why you are here. You must find the strength and wisdom from within to continue on your paths. You are our hope, our inspiration, and the change we wish to see.

In Love and Light,

Nikki Pattillo

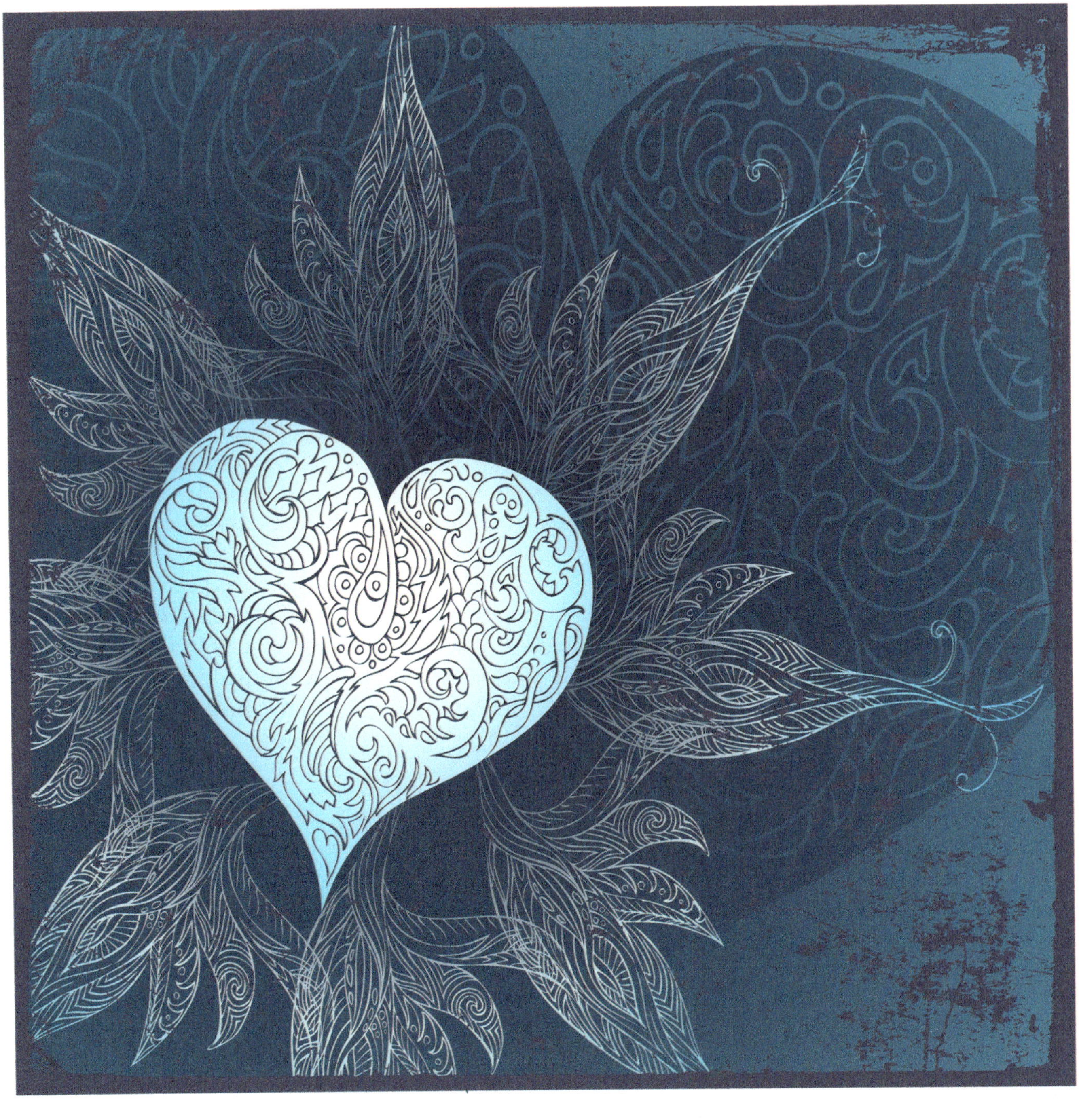

JANUARY

January 1

Bring laughter into your life your life.

Laughter is incredible medicine and one of the most positive things you can experience in life. There is nothing as wonderful as feeling the bubbling of infectious giggles rising within you. Laughter converts negative emotions into positive ones and raises your vibrational frequency.

Today, take every possible moment to laugh and feel happy. This will help bring laughter into your life. What makes you laugh?

January 2

Be in the moment and be happy.

The very purpose of your life is to be happy, and the Angels are always by your side encouraging you to live your life with joy. The more you encourage the happiness of others, the greater your own sense of well-being and happiness will be. Experiencing happy moments is the principle source of a successful life.

Today, make someone smile. It can be a complete stranger or a best friend. Don't think about yesterday or tomorrow, just be in your moment and be happy in that moment.

January 3

Spiritual lessons are everywhere; just open your eyes and see them.

There are spiritual lessons in everything that you do in life, in both good situations and challenging situations. For example, you can turn on your radio and hear a song that is giving you a message you need in your life that particular day such as, "Let it go…" or, you may get laid off from your job only to find out that you have a better job offer the very next week in something you are really interested in.

Find your spiritual lessons this month and write them on your calendar. Nothing is too silly and learning small little lessons can be like a road map to bigger lessons you are learning in your life.

January 4
What am I intended to do?

Your life's purpose or what you are intended to do, contribute, or help with during your life, is important. It can be learned by communicating with your Angels and Guides or by simply allowing your life to be divinely guided by a higher power that helps you so it can unfold into what you are meant to do and who you are meant to be.

Write down things that you are interested in or that you want to help change in this world. These interests will help you figure out what your life's purpose is.

January 5
There are many paths in your life you may or may not know about.

Your Angels are helping to guide you and keep you safe. Trust in the Universe and know that you are never alone. Great things happen when you least expect them, even on a path you may not want or understand as all our experiences are for reasons to help you grow, learn, and understand who you are and why you're here.

Today, don't worry about and accept the unknown in your life. Take a moment to breathe deeply and let go of your worries releasing them into the Universe.

January 6
You are here for a reason.

Do you feel like you are here for a special reason but don't know what it is? That is because you are here on a big mission. What is your big mission? This is a significant event that you have to do in your life—something that has a major impact on humanity or this Earth, including all living and non-living things on it. It could be that you are here to experience hardships in your life and learn and grow from these hardships and then you will have the incredible ability to teach others how to get through theirs. Make it a great adventure to discover what your big mission is. Remember, it may take time for this to unfold and it is important to keep patience in your heart.

Today, write down all experiences that have changed who you are and how they have made you a better person.

January 7
You are a being of higher consciousness.

You are among many lightworkers on this planet who are discovering how to transition to a higher vibrational frequency or higher energy that is similar to your Angels and Guides. You are also transitioning to a new Earth by raising your awareness of what you know and what you are aware of. You can raise your awareness and consciousness through the thoughts, words, and actions you experience in your life and help make this a better world in which to live.

Today, embrace who you are and be who you are meant to be. Know that you are a soul that is here to help change this Earth through your own thoughts, words, actions, and special abilities.

January 8

You are a spiritual being on a human journey.

You are not a human being on a spiritual journey; you are spiritual being on a human journey. This means that you come from spirit to learn and grow in your spiritual lessons, then, go back to spirit to see if you made strides in your spiritual advancement. Everyone makes mistakes, but if you learn from your mistakes, you will grow and become stronger. Everyone struggles and tries to understand spiritual lessons and correct errors so that you can make a positive difference as you walk your spiritual path with joy and happiness.

Think or write about what mistakes you have made in life and how it has changed you for the better.

January 9

Be aware of your consciousness evolution.

Conscious evolution is the process in which you understand and recognize how you are spiritually advancing in life by being aware of and learning your spiritual lessons. As a civilization, conscious evolution is important so we can rediscover our oneness, our common humanity, and how we are all connected.

Write down what knowledge you are gaining in your life and how this knowledge can be shared to help others for you have much to contribute.

A DAY IN SPIRIT

JANUARY

January 10
Karma teaches you responsibility.

Karma is determined by unselfish intentions and motivations; it teaches you how to behave more responsibly and how to be a co–creator of your destiny with your Angels and Guides. The goal of karma is to give you all the experiences that you need to evolve into greater levels of love, joy, awareness, and responsibility. Karma teaches you that you are completely responsible for all circumstances of your life. Karma is like training wheels that keep you on the straight and narrow path until you have mastered your vehicle and can ride freely on your own.

Today, ask yourself if karma has taught you any spiritual lessons? Write these spiritual lessons down.

January 11
Live your life in loving acceptance of all who walk this Earth.

Remember that we belong to each other and are important caretakers of this Earth. We must celebrate our differences to learn and grow from the diversity in our world. Think of how boring this world would be if we all looked the same, talked the same, and acted in the same. It would be like living in a colorless world. Instead, celebrate the variety on Earth and live in oneness and in peace.

Today, think of something you don't agree with and then try and think of that same thing in a new and loving way to show your Angels and Guides that you are living in loving tolerance for all things in life.

January 12
Be a system buster.

You are here to liberate us from our old, outdated ways of doing things by breaking down old systems and paradigms. Outdated systems such as schools, government, and healthcare desperately need to be changed. You help us change this by incarnating into our families and communities and by brining higher levels of consciousness and wisdom to the table. You are here to teach us respect, appreciation, and reverence for all that is and to show us how to care for our home—this planet.

Today, your Angels and Guides say thank you, for being a precious soul that is strong enough to help change this planet, each other, and the ways of doing things for the better.

January 13

Being good and honorable will follow each other in your life.

Being honorable is being ethical and principled and possessing an upright character, one that does not cheat or defraud others. As such, you can be counted on to do what is for the highest good of all at all times, even when nobody is watching you. Remember, that your Angels and Guides are always with you helping to guide you and do what is right and what is good for your soul's evolution and karma.

Observe your thoughts, words, and actions today. Are they positive and benefitting all? Write down how you are good and honorable today.

January 14

Create a loving atmosphere wherever you are.

Creating and living a loving atmosphere in your home and on the planet with your family, friends, neighbors, and even strangers is the foundation for your life. If you feel that you need to change the atmosphere of your life, look to see what you can do create a more positive environment. See the good in all situations and take one step at a time to accept life's many lessons. What you dwell on you create, so create love and happiness in your life.

Today, think of something that brings you joy, sing a song, talk to a tree, breathe more deeply, etc.; and then notice how much better you feel and how this technique affects you.

January 15

Practice Kriyamana karma.

Kriyamana karma is the daily, instant karma created in this life that is worked off immediately. These are debts that are created and then dissipated or balanced in a timely manner. For example, if you do something wrong, you get caught, and you might spend time in jail. It is karma that is right in front of you to decide or act upon and can contribute and/or influence your immediate future karma in an important way.

Today, only you can turn a mess into a message, a test in a testimony, a trial into a triumph, and a victim into victory with your Kriyamana karma.

January 16

Share your knowledge, for it is profound.

You are special and have a certain knowledge that you can't always explain. Share it with others, even if it is a different idea, and you are a bit afraid of what others may think of your ideas. You are on a newer energy grid, that is, you have energy that is more spiritually evolved. You are here to show others more highly evolved ways of living, ways that benefit all, and ways to replace our outdated systems and beliefs. This knowledge is within each of you.

Keep a "good idea" journal. Write down anything and everything that comes into your mind that you think is a great idea, knowledgeable, or that you may need to remember at another time.

January 17

Revive Mother Earth.

Our Earth is being obliterated in the name of progress. As a caretaker of this planet, what can you do today, right at this minute, to help restore Mother Earth and help her flourish again? One step at a time and one day at a time, honor, accept, and fulfill this important responsibility. It's an enormous part of your life's path. Each and every person can make a difference, you are that difference.

Today, think about your role as a caretaker of this planet. What can you do to help the earth?

January 18

Never let fear hold you back.

Fear limits and controls you. Look around. Fear is being used as a tool by so many who have forgotten who they are and why they are here. Recognize it for what it is and never let anyone instill needless fear within you. As you go about your day today, notice people and situations that try to instill unnecessary fear within you. You are truth seekers. See the real truth in all situations and not the fear the media and companies wish you to see to try and control you. One of your special qualities is that you are fearless and you see the truth. Help teach others this amazing quality.

Today, try and see things for the truth of what they really are and not for the information that is being manipulated to instill fear in you. Seek your truth and be fearless in that truth.

A DAY IN SPIRIT

January 19

You are never alone.

You are never alone. Your Angels and Guides are always with you, helping you, guiding you, and giving you encouragement every day of your life. They are sending you messages of love while you learn your spiritual lessons. Place your hands over your heart and acknowledge their presence and feel your entire being flooded with their loving energy.

Know you are loved and receive this love being sent to you by your Angels and Guides.

January 20

Give up something.

Some people judge success by what they had to give up in order to achieve this success. Giving up implies that you give someone else something you really like, but it is not. What can you give up today or donate to someone that will benefit from it without feeling any loss? There are so many choices: time, clothing, your understanding of a subject in which someone needs tutoring, a kind word, etc.

Today, raise your vibrational frequency by doing something for someone else. Make a list of what you shared or are willing to give up.

January 21

It's all about love.

Our issues are always about love—love that we wish we received, love that we felt we deserved and never got, or love that was somehow lost. By keeping love in your heart at all times, you will be living in a higher state of awareness and consciousness about this subject, which will help you to heal. You are never alone and are always loved by your Angels and Guides not matter who you are or what you have done in your life. This love surrounds your entire being at all times.

Today be aware that you are loved and also aware of those who need love and reach out to them.

January 22

Angels are real.

Sometimes the most real things in this world are those we can't see, such as Angels. They are with us every day of our life giving us messages of hope and inspiration. Don't ever doubt that a team of Angels surrounds you each and every day of your life. Take a few minutes today to acknowledge your Angels and tell them thank you for being with you. Order an Angel if you want to or if you are in a difficult situation that you need help with. They are countless in their numbers and are always here to love, support, and guide you.

Meditate for a few moments and ask your Angels to give you a message. Write that message down.

January 23

Give a little bit of your time and effort to someone else.

Every week or every month, give a small amount of your time to a cause that is important to you. Whether it is posting support on Facebook or Twitter or dropping off something to someone in need in your community, you should make an effort to help others somewhere in this world. The Angels say the fastest way to raise your vibrational frequency is by being in service to others.

Take a moment to help someone or an organization in need today. Write a big Angel with a smiley face in your journal for they are proud of you.

January 24

Do you know the Law of Love?

If you don't know love, if you haven't felt love, then you will never know the core element of creation. The Law of Love states, "You shall love your neighbor as yourself." Who is your neighbor? Everyone is your neighbor. The Law of Love really means, "Love all people as yourself" because everyone is us, and we are everyone.

Today, ask what is one way you can love someone as you would love yourself? Keep a list of how you can do this.

January 25
Angels surround you.

Without exception, all individuals have Angels around them constantly, who are eager and excited at the opportunity to communicate with them. Usually you have one to three Guardian Angels assigned to you your whole life or for many lifetimes, but additional Angels will come and go as you work on your spiritual lessons. Angels were created with one purpose—to love and to serve without conditions. In doing so, Angels hold a focus of pure love throughout the Universe and are able to set up a resonance for the vibration of pure love wherever and whenever it is needed.

Today, think of or write down one instance that you knew an Angel was with you or helped and guided you.

January 26
Live life with happiness and forgiveness.

Live life with happiness and forgiveness, and love will soar into your life. If you are not happy, then look at your life and find one thing you can do to bring a smile to yourself or someone else. Place forgiveness in your heart if you cannot find a happy moment. You will be walking as if you are an Angel on Earth by doing this and in the process, it will help you find your happiness.

Today, forgive yourself if you feel you need forgiveness and forgive others around you as well. Then feel the happiness that you are meant to experience come into your life.

January 27
Karma lives in the law of cause and effect.

The law of cause and effect basically states that for every movement of energy that takes the form of an image, feeling, desire, belief, expectation, or action, there is a corresponding effect. For this reason, the law of cause and effect influences every aspect of your karma. In order for you to make the most of the law of cause and effect, you must live consciously and recognize that you are the creator of your own reality and therefore your own destiny.

Try and make it a karmic goal today to ensure that you link your actions (the cause) with their results (the effect). A positive cause, a positive effect. A negative cause, a negative effect. For example, if you go to bed early, you will wake up rested. If you go to bed late, you will feel tired and grumpy.

A DAY IN SPIRIT

January 28

Your Guardian Angels are not separate from you.

Your Guardian Angels are dedicated to you, travel with you everywhere you go, and are with you at all times. They have made an agreement with your soul to assist you in completing any of the tasks or lessons you have decided to undertake. You are never alone and they are by your side, loving you, guiding you, and showing you the way to peace and happiness.

Ask your Angel today for help with a certain problem or issue that is challenging you. Write down any messages or help you receive from them.

January 29

You are a teacher of conscious awareness.

Every thought that you have, every word that you speak either adds to or takes away from the light of humanity. Everything that you think and/or say about yourself, whether it is silently to yourself or aloud to others, either adds to or takes away from the light of humanity. Everything that you think or say to or about others, whether it is silently to yourself or aloud to others, either adds to or takes away from the light of humanity. There are no insignificant thoughts or words. Each one has energy and an effect.

Before you speak today, stop and consider the power of your thoughts, words, and actions. Be a teacher by being a light and spreading your light. Write down how you are doing this.

January 30

Your power creates a miracle.

You have the power to manifest anything you want or need, including a miracle. If it is for the highest good for all involved, it will happen. Manifesting an iceberg while living in the tropics may not happen. Make your miracle achievable and visualize it happening in your life. Miracles happen every day and you have the ability to create those miracles.

Try and manifest a small miracle today. Write down anything amazing or unusual that happened that may lead up to that miracle coming to fruition.

January 31

Always trust in the Universe.

Know that you are loved and being guided in the best possible ways towards your greatest potential, spiritual lessons, and life purpose. The Universe is at your beck and call to help you. You only need to ask for it. Release all your worries and fears to the Universe, it will help heal and guide you to the best opportunity or situation for you to be in.

Throw a problem you are having out to the Universe and ask for help. Write down what happens in the days and weeks to come to prove to yourself that trusting in the Universe really works.

JANUARY

A DAY IN SPIRIT

FEBRUARY

February 1

Live your life in forgiveness.

Forgiveness is living in a state of grace, and you are truly happy when you forgive everyone in your life. Living in forgiveness is probably one of the most difficult things to do as it requires a tremendous amount of strength.

Today, ask who you need to forgive in your life and truly forgive and let go.

February 2

Love is all you need.

Send your thoughts and words through your heart chakra before you speak. This way you are speaking with kindness and through love. Love is the answer and all you need.

Practice channeling your thoughts and speaking with kindness, gentleness, and love today.

February 3

Give to others and give to the earth.

When you pick up trash off the street, you are in service to the earth. When you listen to others, speak kind words to them, send them loving thoughts, or help them with your actions, you are in service to humanity. Being in service raises your vibrational frequency and allows you to live your life with compassion and awareness. You are a beautiful and precious part of humanity.

What act of service or kindness will you do today?

February 4

Be grateful.

Everything that happens in your life, whether it appears to be good or challenging, is an opportunity for you to learn great spiritual lessons. Be grateful. Be aware today of any spiritual lessons and opportunities for growth in both positive and demanding situations as there is an opportunity to spiritually advance in both situations. Then say, "Thanks!"

Be grateful today and know that there are spiritual lessons to be learned every day of your life. Write down three things that you are grateful for.

February 5

Practice empathy.

Today try to place yourself in the shoes of another person. Any person—loved ones, co-workers, people you meet on the street, etc. To the extent that you can really try to understand what it is like to be them and experience what they are going through and why they do what they do. Sometimes people are in so much pain that they lash out at others. Remember times when you have felt and acted this way. Honor all individuals in their current circumstances; do not judge them, for there is much you do not know.

Today, choose to live your life in loving acceptance of all for you don't know how easy or difficult others' spiritual lessons are. This is how you practice empathy.

February 6

Karma is a non-punishing force.

It is very important for you to understand that karma is not a system of punishment put in place by a higher authority. The common misconception is that the laws of karma operate in such a manner as to punish you for your so-called wrongdoings. The punishment is always self inflicted from a karmic point of view. Karma acts on a living entity based on its previous actions. This counteraction allows you to be placed in a situation where you understand why your previous choices and actions were mistakes. You learn best through experience, and this is what karma does—it puts you in places and circumstances where you experience spiritual lessons first hand.

Today, work on creating positive karma in your life. Write down how you can do this.

February 7

Practice compassion.

Once you try to understand another person and feel what they're going through, look to see what you can do to help them in their time of suffering. You may not be able to end their suffering if it is their path, but a caring word or deed from you may somehow ease their suffering in some way. Remember that pain and suffering come in many forms and levels. Look around and see what you can do to help others in any small way you can.

Take a small action to ease someone's suffering today. Write that good deed down and be proud of what you have done to practice compassion.

February 8

Practice the Golden Rule.

How do you wish to be treated? The Golden Rule doesn't really mean that you should treat others exactly as you'd want them to treat you; it means that you should try to imagine how they wish to be treated and do that. Try to put yourself in their shoes. Then ask yourself how you think they want to be treated.

Today, practice the Golden Rule and write down what that means to you.

February 9

Be kind to everyone, and you will find true happiness.

Be kind to others, even those who are not kind to you, and you will find true happiness. You are living in your light and spreading your light when you are kind to all and not only is this good karma, it also makes your Angels and Guides very proud of you.

What act of kindness will you do today?

A DAY IN SPIRIT

February 10

Keep everything in balance.

The Universe exists in a state of balance, as should you. You can do almost anything you wish, but should always do it in moderation—never in excess and always in consciousness of all living and non–living things in this world. Anything in excess can become addictive, which drains energy. Staying balanced in your life allows you to keep and maintain a higher vibrational frequency.

Today, ask yourself what needs balancing in your life?

February 11

Your Angels have been created to serve, love, hold, and support you.

Angels have been created to serve, love, hold, and support those to whom they are assigned, and those who ask for angelic support. Angels can be found in every corner of the Universe and are countless in their numbers. They are everywhere awaiting your permission to help. A request for Angels is simple. Just say, "Dear Angels, please send me an Angel that specializes in this situation. Thank you."

Every day, you can ask for an Angel to go wherever you go, do whatever you do, and help however they can help. You just need ask.

February 12

We are all one.

You have been all colors, races, shapes, and sizes through reincarnation and karma. Try to see each person as an individual soul here on our planet learning spiritual lessons not just a person in a physical body. We are all one, and if you hurt someone else, you are only hurting yourself through karmic debt.

Take a deep breath and visualize our Earth as one global community working together towards higher awareness and higher levels of consciousness. What is one word you would use to describe this?

February 13
Praise or compliment another person.

Sometimes people need just a kind word from another person, even from a stranger. A few kind words can literally change someone's life. Notice the good in others—it can be their smile, hair, hat, clothes, the way they walk, or how they treat others. Compliment them based on your observations. Make eye contact as you compliment them. If you do this sincerely, you will truly "make their day!"

Be kind whenever possible as the possibilities in acts of kindness in your life know no bounds.

February 14
It is the Law of Love which governs our nature.

Love is always the answer and all that is. The Angels ask that you never cause pain to others in any way. Love all who walk this Earth and be sure to have love and faith in your own self.

What act of love can you do today?

February 15
Service is a great way to create positive karma.

Service is a great way to create positive karma. The process is something like this: as you serve, you draw energy to yourself. By giving energy, you receive energy in return. Create good energy through service; in return, you and the world will be blessed in so many unbelievable ways.

What act of service big or small, can or will you do today?

February 16
Practice Prarabdha karma.

Prarabdha karma is considered fructifying karma or the idea of an "action beginning and being set in motion." This is the portion of your karma that your soul works on in your present life. If you work down your agreed–upon debt in this lifetime, then more past debts surface and can be worked on as well. This is how Prarabdha karma gets dissolved.

Remember, it is said that love is the strongest of all life's passions. Through your soul, it reaches your heart and through your heart it reaches your mind and this, can help your Prarabdha karma.

February 17
Stay connected to humanity.

We share an energetic field here on Earth. It links us all together and this is why a shift in consciousness moves through us all, and changes life as we feel it and see it. We were made to be strong with each other, to interlink into divinity through the intertwining of our hearts and souls. When alone, we can find each other. Through each other, we can find ourselves and this helps connect us.

Write down a few things connecting you to other people on our Earth.

February 18
You are able to fulfill your purpose just by being the radiant soul that you are.

There is no way that you cannot be who you are as a soul, and so your purpose is unfolding with every breath that you take. You are a part of the living web of life here on Earth, and each soul within that web is a part of the whole, unique, and divine plan for all of humanity.

Consciously hold your loving light today knowing you are special and here for a reason.

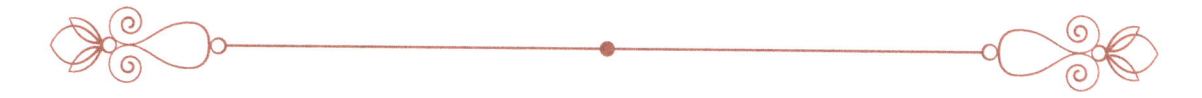

A DAY IN SPIRIT

February 19

When discovering who you are as a soul, a new freedom emerges within your heart.

Your heart has many beautiful and wonderful secrets held within it waiting to be discovered. With this discovery is the freedom of the soul, the freedom of love, and the freedom to be and live in beauty and grace because this who you truly are.

How can you share beauty and grace with someone today?

February 20

Your Angels and Guides are always with you during your journey.

Angels are always within your touch, sight, and hearing as they offer gentle reminders of who you are, why you're here, and how to find your way in this crazy life on Earth. You are always on the right path when you walk with love in your heart just as your Angels and Guides do.

Was there a time today when you felt you received guidance? What was that guidance?

February 21

Be on the right path.

Being on the right path is remembering the power of forgiveness because forgiveness is important when dealing with old emotions that can be carried around within your heart. These lower vibrational energies may block or slow your abilities to deal with life's day–to–day issues in positive and constructive ways and keep you looping in the same pattern until your spiritual lesson are learned. Remember, who you are and why you're here to help you stay on the right path in your life.

Practice forgiveness at least once today and write down how that is helping you stay on the path in your life.

February 22

Continue to move forward in your life, regardless of the circumstances.

For your spirit, it is important that you move forward in your life, regardless of the circumstances. Clear your emotional bodies and/or auras and free some space in your heart to work on your path in life. When you do this, your spirit will overflow with an abundance of love.

Today, clear your emotions and set the intention that you can move forward no matter what obstacles lay in your path.

February 23

Great opportunities lie within you.

Great opportunities lie within you, even buried deeply beneath old scars and betrayals. You can waste much energy on old feelings and emotions that don't serve you anymore. Living a life in awareness and consciousness of these issues, embracing all situations for what they are, and learning to grow from them will open further opportunities for you

Today, recognize the great gifts you offer this planet we call Earth. What opportunities lie within you because of these gifts?

February 24

Forgiveness is the foundation of all spiritual work.

Forgiveness is the foundation of all spiritual work and growth because it is by living in awareness of forgiveness that you can truly know your own life's journey and purpose. Forgiveness is not a process of giving something to another person who may not deserve anything in return. It is a process of turning your energy inward and using the power of love to look at relationships within yourself and others. Only then can you understand how important forgiveness is in your spiritual growth.

Who can you forgive today that you thought was "unforgivable?"

February 25

Love is the healing energy that binds all of humanity.

The issues that seem to defy forgiveness and your healing energy are always about love: love that you never received, love offered but rejected or betrayed, or love used as manipulation or control. There are many ways in which healing issues are tied to love. By tying up your spiritual energy reserves in old issues, you are limiting the vibrational level of love available in your present life. Find and be the love.

Now is the time to begin searching your heart to discover the love that surrounds you.

February 26

Emerge each day with great clarity and direct purpose.

Do not be overshadowed by yesterday's old, outdated energies. Instead, remain clear and alive in your current or present moment. Ask your higher power to accept each day anew without any burdens of previous troubles or hurts. Each morning and evening, review any old emotions or hurts from the day before that you are carrying around and work through them, letting them go, and allowing your spiritual light to shine through.

Start your day today with clarity and purpose.

February 27

Recognize great spiritual lessons while they are happening.

Many of the great spiritual lessons that your experiences teach you are not recognized while you are in the midst of these lessons. Only later do you see the profound teachings these experiences offered you. These lessons can help you immensely when future strife and loss enter your life. They will not eliminate the pain, but they can give you greater strength, deeper hope, and clearer understanding with things that are occurring. They can also give you courage to stay in the turmoil and to trust that you will survive these struggles and not be destroyed by them—instead, learn and draw strength from them.

If you have spiritual lessons every day, what have you learned today?

A DAY IN SPIRIT

February 28

Don't judge others.

You don't know others' spiritual lessons or their spiritual evolutionary paths, so you must never judge anyone because it lowers your vibrational frequency and leaves you without compassion. Keeping compassion in your hearts for all living and non–living things is important since compassion is yet another powerful emotion that heals us all and excels our spiritual lessons and growth.

Today, change your judgment towards others to compassion for their difficult spiritual lessons they are going through. Who can you do this with?

February 29

Lead with your heart.

You have the most amazing and beautiful gift within your soul and this is your heart. All thoughts that you think, all words that you speak, and all actions that you take should be filtered through this wondrous part of you. It's not okay for people to take advantage of you and you should always stand up for yourself, but you should also live your life in kindness and this means leading your life with your heart.

Feel your beating heart and feel how it is filled with an endless amount of love, kindness, and forgiveness.

A DAY IN SPIRIT

MARCH

March 1

Let go of the past.

One of the hardest things to do in life is to let go of the past. Dwelling on issues for too long can close your heart chakra and keep you from being fully present in your current moment. When you are not fully present in the now, you are not living your life to the fullest. Without letting go of the past, you are not free and your energy fields get tied up running old programs, blocking you from receiving love and knowledge from the Universe.

Today, let go of yesterday and the past and live in this happy moment right now.

March 2

Embark on a path of self-discovery, self-healing, and spiritual growth.

Your decision to embark on a path of self-discovery, self-healing, and spiritual growth is one that requires great courage, perseverance, and determination. There is truth to your purpose, and this truth always lies within your heart chakra. Often you have forgotten about opening your heart chakra to receive guidance from your Angels, Guides, and the Universe itself while on your path. Remember to do this and your road in life will be easier.

How can you remind yourself to open your heart chakra on a daily basis while embarking on your path in life?

March 3

Have the courage to face your inner self.

The mark of great warriors or masters is that they are willing time and again to face their own darkness, their own demons, and have the courage to face their inner selves. This requires stripping down the layers that have built upon false foundations and being who you truly are. You have the strength and courage to do this—to find the beautiful soul within yourself.

Today, feel your inner strength and courage through Divine spirit. What have you been courageous about lately?

March 4

Through courage, perseverance, and love for self, you can heal.

Through courage, perseverance, and love for self, you can make the commitment to heal and evolve through your spirit and help others to do the same. Know you are a strong warrior and your Angels are always with you to strengthen your courage and ability to heal.

Look up to the Universe and feel strength, wisdom, and courage being downloaded to you. What does this feel like?

March 5

Know what your life's purpose is.

It is important not to waste a life by not knowing what your life's purpose is or how you can contribute to humanity. Being of service and holding loving energies wherever you go are examples of global life purposes. If you find your life purpose early in your life, you can consciously work on the spiritual issues related to this. Trust that your Angels and Guides will be assisting and guiding you with your life purpose, whether you consciously realize it or not.

Ask your Angels for help if you don't know why you are here or how you are to help. The answer may be revealed in unusual ways.

March 6

Being strong does not necessarily imply a powerful body.

Being strong does not necessarily imply a powerful body or great intellect; great strength implies the power you have within your spirit. Overcoming obstacles in life sometimes requires you to reach deep down within and tap into your spiritual strength. This source is limitless and you only have to reach within to feel it.

Today, draw strength from your spirit and not from your physical prowess. What gives your spirit strength?

March 7

Your Guardian Angels are not separate from you.

Your Guardian Angels are not separate from you, they are dedicated to you and travel with you everywhere you go and are with you at all times. They have made an agreement with your soul to assist you in completing any of the tasks or lessons you have decided to undertake in your life. Some are created from the same essence as you and will be with you during many lifetimes.

Your spiritual connection with your Guardian Angel is very real. Name a time you felt your Guardian Angel was with you.

March 8

It is truly the healers of the world who choose the most difficult of paths.

It is truly the healers of the world who choose the most difficult of paths, and this is a gift to humanity. It is a gift because often healers or teachers will take on additional hardships and will transmute this energy to more positive circumstances. By doing this, they can show us the way to shift our own energies with similar situations. They take on these hardships and shift them in order to spiritually share the burden that humanity carries. In a way, we are all healers in this world.

Ask yourself, what experiences have you healed from that you can share to help others' heal through your lessons?

March 9

You are on a great journey.

For your soul, coming to Earth is like traveling away from your home to a foreign land. Some things seem familiar, but most seem strange until you have a chance to get used to them. Some of the seemingly unforgiving conditions found on this tough playground we call Earth are a definite challenge. Your home on the spiritual plane is a place of absolute peace, total acceptance, and complete love where you are able to instantly manifest anything and everything you want or need at any given moment. As your soul leaves the spiritual realm, you no longer have easy access to these unique gifts, and this can be a tough adjustment.

Today, recognize that you are here on Earth for not just spiritual lessons, but, to also have fun.

A DAY IN SPIRIT

March 10

You must learn to cope with intolerance, anger, and sadness while searching for joy and love.

As you progress along your path in life, you must not lose your integrity, sacrifice goodness for survival, or acquire superior or inferior attitudes to those around you. You know that living in an imperfect world will help you to appreciate the true meaning of perfection. This is done by living in loving acceptance of our differences and commonalities as one humanity living on the same Earth.

Today, live in loving acceptance and tolerance of the differences that surround you.

March 11

You are blessed with a special gift.

Each of you is blessed with unique lessons and special gifts in life that can be used to help make the world a kinder, more loving, just, and beautiful world in which to live. Discover your gifts and share these gifts with others.

Ask yourself what gifts you have within you today. Write down how these gifts can help others.

March 12

Karma teaches you spirituality.

The purpose of living in spiritual awareness is to create an Earth where you will rediscover your oneness, your common humanity. All of you need to thrive and be respected for who or what you are. Earth is a place where you can learn to respect the similarities and the differences between yourself and the planet through your spirituality and live in loving tolerance of those differences.

Today, understand that great beauty, wisdom, and opportunity are within you while living a life in consciousness and awareness through your spirituality.

March 13

Live by the Golden Rule.

Being a spiritual person means living by The Golden Rule, "Do unto others as you would have them do unto you." Live each day by the Golden Rule and allow each day of your life to be expressed in a positive way that will enlighten your path with goodness, raise your vibrational frequency, and live within higher levels of consciousness.

Live the Golden Rule and understand that everyone has a different path in life that should be respected. Write down what one of your own Golden Rules are.

March 14

Live without judgment.

To implement the teaching of spirituality is to practice what you preach and live without judgment. You don't know what others' life purposes or spiritual lessons are. You must remember that things are not always what they appear to be—nor are people always who they appear to us to be. Withholding from judgment in all situations is practicing spiritual understanding and extending love to others. This is a great platform on which to stand so you can live a life with grace, compassion, kindness, inclusion, and love, which aids you in your spiritual evolution.

Today, wish someone well who you might judge.

March 15

You are sitting on a spiritual gold mine.

You are sitting on a spiritual gold mine called "your lifetime." It is filled with enriching experiences that allow you to grow and learn and expand. Not all of these experiences may seem happy at the time, but if you trust that you can come through them as a more aware and conscious individual, then you will spread enormous light on this planet. In the past you may not have always been aware of some of your spiritual experiences, but now that you know about them, begin to pay greater attention to the events in your life as they lead you along your path.

Be aware and conscious of the greatness that you hold within your spirit.

March 16

Anchor love in your heart.

Spiritual lessons are usually quite simple and are frequently about love and forgiveness; therefore, it is important to anchor love in your heart while learning your lessons. Watching for patterns and looking for the spiritual lessons your soul agreed to experience becomes easier when you keep your heart in the right place and anchored in love.

Today, keep your heart anchored in love for all people in all walks of life.

March 17

You have great inner strength.

Strength does not come from how intelligent you are or how many push–ups you can do. True inner strength comes from the power of your spirit. Great teachers of the world, such as Buddha, derived their strength and inspiration not from muscle or intellect but from faith. Buddha spoke a language that went straight to people's hearts. The great spiritual teachers of the world speak and connect to you through your heart chakra and ask you to have strength through this faith.

Recognize how much inner strength you have, not through physical strength but strength that comes from faith. Make a list of what makes you strong in your life?

March 18

Live with a golden compass in your heart.

There is a spiritual compass within you that helps guide and direct you in your life. It is very powerful and guided by your Angels and Guides and your own soul. Be still and listen, watch for your spiritual lessons, and learn from these lessons by the day–to–day guidance from this golden compass.

Today, look within and find the golden compass contained within your heart. What is the directional heading of that compass?

A DAY IN SPIRIT

March 19

Strive to become better than you already are.

To learn your spiritual lessons, you must strive in your spiritual evolution to become the true you, not just the human clothing you wear. You were given what might seem to you to be an imperfect body in one or more way but instead it is the perfect body to fulfill your life's purpose. Rather than concentrate only on this particular body in this specific life, focus on your spiritual growth and the evolution of your soul.

Know that you can spiritually grow each and every day through awareness of whom you are and why you are here and in this way, you can strive to become better.

March 20

There are great lessons to be learned while you are on Earth.

There are many great lessons to be learned while you are here. Earth appeals to your soul because of the kinship you have for others like yourself while struggling here. You compete and collaborate at the same time. Humans can be egocentric but vulnerable. Some can appear to be mean and yet have a great capacity for kindness. Sometimes you are weak and other times you are courageous. There are times when a tug-of-war exists within you to be strong and always do the right thing in life or take an easier road. When you awaken your passion to do what is right in life, you spark others to do the same and send a wave of benevolence throughout the world.

Today, try to do what is right and to help others do what is right so spiritual lessons can be learned and spiritual advancement can be made.

March 21

You have a great capacity for kindness within you.

This capacity for kindness grows and evolves within you when you practice random acts of kindness. When you experience hard times, you learn the value of kindness and this gives you the ability to share it with others. Seeing others go through pain and suffering often evokes a need within us to help them in some way. Doing so then creates great beauty and peace on Earth.

What act of kindness can you practice today?

March 22
Overcome fear.

There are many fears to overcome during your life here on this Earth. The unknown often creates fear. When you don't know or understand someone and/or have heard "things" about that person, you sometimes fear and avoid that person or look down upon that individual. Often if you have an opportunity to get to know that person or situation, your fear dwindles and disappears. There is great diversity on Earth that can awaken the fear within us. When you keep love in your hearts and live by the Law of Oneness—for we are all truly connected to each other and to our Earth—fear will have no hold on you.

Today, honor others' diversity and uniqueness and know that you are placed here by a higher power and are never to keep fear in your heart.

March 23
Everything you do in your home is reflected in your life and in your body.

Everything within your body, heart, and spirit is seen in your home, your room, and in your life. There is a spiritual law that states, "Your body is the home of your spirit, so it is sacred, a temple to house the Divine." Your house is the home of the sacred body, the temple of your soul, and so it is an extension of Spirit's sacred space.

Keep your home in balance just as you keep your mind, body, and spirit in balance. Write down what is in your room that may need cleaning or balancing.

March 24
Intent is action.

You can intend to do anything, and your intent is important. However, unless the intent is followed with action, the intent will not come to fruition. For example, you may intend to get fit but spend your time watching TV, eating pizza, and drinking Coke. You have intention, but your actions do not confirm or create the intention; therefore, you must use actions to create or manifest what you want. If action turns knowledge into wisdom, then consciousness is intent with action. You can be mindful of something, but unless you put action into that thought, it is not conscious and consciousness helps raise your vibrational frequency.

Today, put action behind your intentions.

March 25
One step at a time.

To achieve any goal in life, it should be broken down into a number of smaller steps. If you have many small successes, this can lead to larger successes. If you aim for large goals too quickly, you may fail. Remember that every journey begins with a single step, then a second and a third, and as many steps required until you reach your destination. You should reward and praise yourself for all your successes, however big or small they are. What you dwell on you create, so manifest many goals in life and achieve success one step at a time.

Ask yourself, what is the biggest goal or dream you have in your life and what is the first step towards that goal or dream?

March 26
Practice Sanchita karma.

Sanchita karma is the sum total or accumulated actions karma. It is the accumulated result of all your actions from all your past lifetimes. In every moment of every day, you either are adding to or reducing this type of karma. Sanchita karma is the vast store of karma accumulated in all previous births that has yet to be resolved. This is your total cosmic debt, and it is waiting to be fulfilled in your future births. So unless and until the Sanchita karma of a soul is cleared, it will remain with you in each new physical body in order to exhaust its balance.

Today, learn new ways to think and see things so you can master a new way to be those things and clear out your Sanchita karma.

March 27
Everything is energy.

Everything is energy; everything in the Universe is made up of tiny molecules that vibrate at a specific frequency. The Law of Attraction states that like attracts like. For example, when strumming a guitar string, the vibration of that specific string will sound throughout the guitar and even begin to vibrate the other strings next to it. Likewise, when striking a tuning fork and placing it next to another tuning fork, it will also begin to audibly vibrate at the same frequency.

Today, keep your energy/vibrational frequency at high levels and see what will be attracted to you and know you are affecting those around you in a positive way by this higher frequency.

A DAY IN SPIRIT

March 28

You are a beacon.

Every day of your life, you are interacting with the vibrational frequencies of people and places around you. Likewise, you are projecting your vibrational frequencies. Being peaceful is a great example of this since peace begins from within. If you are peaceful, others will feel this peace and be at peace around you. If you love and forgive yourself, then you will easily love and forgive others.

Work on being a beacon of light today that projects positive energy in all directions. What does your beacon look like?

March 29

Feel peace within your heart.

If you feel peaceful within your own heart, then others around you will start to feel and match this peaceful vibrational frequency. You can affect many people by keeping love and peace in your hearts at all times. This is how one person can and does change the world for the better. It all starts with what you think, what you feel, what you say, and what you focus on and give energy to.

Ask yourself what are you feeling in your heart today?

March 30

Manifest what is for your highest good.

You can manifest most anything that is for your highest good. You must consider the laws that govern your world when you are trying to manifest something. You all have your paths for this lifetime. How you walk your path is up to you; however, because of the law of free will, you cannot manifest someone else's actions or bend the will of another to match your desires. Your creations must be for the highest good of all concerned, including yourself.

Manifest one small thing today. Write down what that is.

March 31, 2016

Be happy.

If you decided you were happy no matter what brand of clothes you wore, what kind of car, home, job, relationship, cereal, makeup, jewelry, vacation, or life you had, your consciousness and that of the entire Universe would shift. Most advanced souls can manifest these things but care little about them. Instead, being in service to humanity is what makes them happy. Wake up each morning feeling happy and blessed that you are here in service to humanity, no matter what materialistic possessions you have.

Today, let your happiness shine a light on all. What are 3 things that make you happy?

MARCH

A DAY IN SPIRIT

APRIL

April 1

Clear negative energy from your life to help with abundance.

It is important to clear negative energy or energy of a lower vibrational frequency from life when you are manifesting abundance. You can do this by simply meditating and asking your Angels to clear all energies that are not for your highest good. It is that simple.

Clear your negative by saying, "Dear higher power, please bless me with energy, to bring healing and balance to my complete being physically, emotionally, and spiritually."

April 2

Bad people are good when you are good enough.

As Lao Tzu says, "I find good people good, and I find bad people good when I am good enough." Remember, you are all affecting the world at every moment. Your actions and state of mind matter because you are so deeply interconnected with everyone and everything. Goodness, like laughter, can be contagious. Working on your own consciousness and your own path in life is the most important thing that you can do at any moment as an evolving spirit.

What can you do today to spread goodness?

April 3

You share an energetic field with all that is.

On Earth you hear the phrase "The Web of Life," which explains how we are all interconnected and dependent upon one another. You are made to be strong with each other and interlink to divinity through the intertwining of your hearts and souls. When alone, you can find each other. Through each other, you can find yourself and this helps connect you. There is an energetic field that links everyone and everything. This is why when you have a shift in consciousness and become more loving and aware of sharing that love; it touches all, and completes the divine circuit of life.

What will you do today to keep this energetic circuit strong?

April 4
Emotional pain can bring productivity.

At times, the most emotionally painful lives can be the most creative and the most productive ones. Emotional pain and turmoil can make you more insightful and bring you closer to your spiritual lessons and closer to each other. Through your pain, you can connect to each other by respecting life. You share your common humanity by being tolerant and generous amongst yourself and each other.

Think about what you have gone through in your life and how it can help you connect to others who are going through similar circumstances.

April 5
Karma teaches you to learn your lessons.

The main reason for reincarnating is to learn your spiritual lessons and to advance spiritually. Reincarnation and karma are thus interrelated. However, this does not apply to those who choose to reincarnate to teach others and help them to grow spiritually. Before you reincarnate, you choose the circumstances, parents, social conditions, and situations into which you are born in order to give you the ideal conditions for learning the lessons that you have set out to learn in this lifetime. This means that your current family genetics and psychological environments are not mainly responsible for your psychological makeup. They are only the vehicles for the expression of your soul and serve to bring about the interplay of factors required for the natural unfolding of your karmic circumstances.

What karmic lessons are you learning today?

April 6
Talk to your Angels every day.

Angels are spirits without bodies, who possess superior intelligence, gigantic strength, and surpassing holiness. They are countless in their number and flock around the Universe in their millions, helping all spiritual beings that ask for their love and guidance. All you need to do is ask for help or order an Angel and they will be there.

Know that your Angels are listening to you, talk to them each day, and ask for help and guidance and then await their help.

April 7

You and you alone can help create a new and better Earth.

You can help create a better Earth by living in higher consciousness. This is a place where all living beings can thrive and be respected for who they are—one where we honor and enjoy each other's similarities and differences—a place of celebrating the incredible diversity that characterizes your oneness and makes life an adventure in consciousness. In a peaceful world you live in loving tolerance of similarities and differences that you have with each other. Peace must also be made within yourself in order to make peace in the world and to connect with humanity.

Today, celebrate the incredible diversity that characterizes your oneness and makes life an adventure in consciousness.

April 8

Your thoughts and words should come from unconditional love.

When your thoughts and words come from a space of unconditional love and non-judgment, they spread a light and increase the light and vibrational frequency on the planet. When they come from fear or anger, they take away from the light. Your thoughts and words make a difference; each one is important. Even the smallest judgment or thought has an effect. Each person is as important as another in spreading the light and connecting to others.

Today, be conscious of the thoughts you think, words you say, and actions that you take.

April 9

You are here to build and spread the light for all of humanity.

You are love's light and here to spread that light throughout the world. Focus your energy on bringing more light into your life and the life of others. Each of you is important to the task that you have come to do. The result of your energy is continuously manifested all around you. Take this power of love that has been taught to you and use it wisely. When you do, you create heaven on Earth for yourself and for all of humanity.

Today, focus your energy on what you want and bring all positively manifested light into your life.

A DAY IN SPIRIT

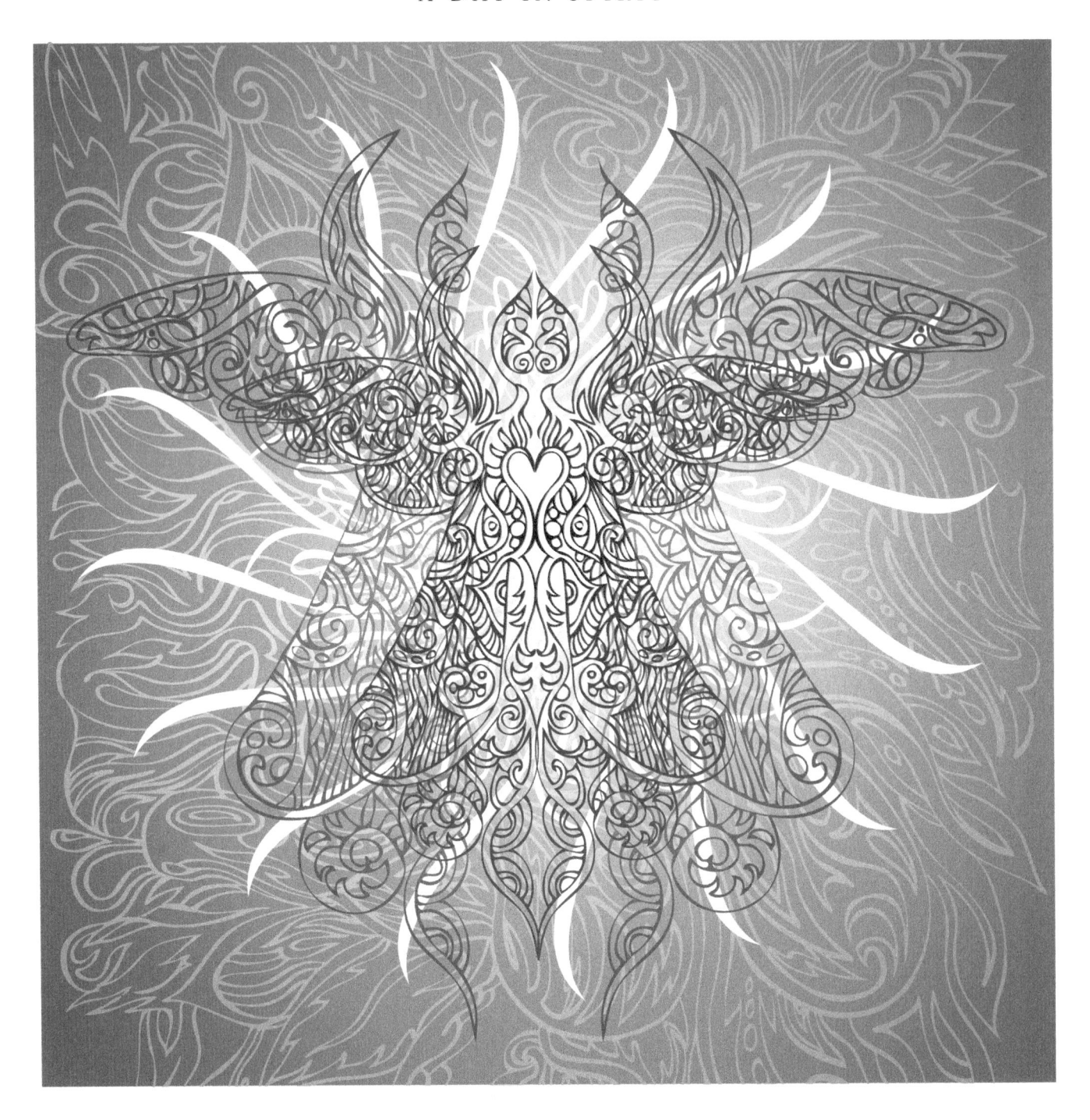

APRIL

April 10

Belief creates.

What you dwell on, you create. How you perceive the Universe is shaped by your beliefs, and if you believe you are in a hurry, then everyone else appears to be moving slowly. Through belief and positive thought, you can create or manifest anything you want or need for your higher good or the higher good of others. You should always believe in your abilities and yourself. If you believe in your spirit, you will succeed.

Realize today that if you can combine the power of belief with that of manifestation, you can bring anything into your reality.

April 11

Hold the light not only within yourself, but also upon those who will not or do not know how to hold the light on themselves.

As aware and conscious spiritual beings, it is important to hold the light of love within yourself and for others until they can do so themselves. You made an agreement before you were born to fulfill a purpose and how you were going to live your life to achieve that purpose and help humanity. You don't know what these agreements are for others or the role they chose to play in the Divine plan of things; however, if they are in your life, you have agreed to work with them.

What will you do today to hold the light both on yourself and others?

April 12

The path of awakening leads to the heart of the Universe.

Your path is your journey through life, which is wider and longer than any single earthly lifetime. On this path you learn who you are, what you are doing here, and where you are going. Others may point the way, but it is you who actually obtains knowledge and develops the wisdom needed to awaken your inner consciousness and awareness. You can do this by living your life in awareness and consciousness of who you are and why you are really here

Write down what your life's purpose is and what your path in life may be.

April 13

Your Angels are spirits without bodies.

Your Angels are spirits without bodies who possess superior intelligence, gigantic strength, and surpassing holiness. Angels are composed of ethereal matter, thus allowing them to take on whichever physical form best suits their immediate needs to work with you on your spiritual lessons in your life. They are the essence of love and joy and stem from the heart of God. They are countless in their number and flock around the Universe in their millions, helping all spiritual beings that ask for their love and guidance.

Call on your Angels with something you need help with today.

April 14

You have free will, use it wisely.

Here on Earth, you have free will. This means that you have chosen to gain your experiences through many lifetimes and many varied forms of existence. Your Angels are created to counterbalance any energies or actions that move in the opposite direction to love during times of free will so that you will remember your true spiritual purpose.

Recognize that love is all around you every day of your life; you only need to open your eyes to see it, feel it, and experience it through your free will.

April 15

Being on the right spiritual path is about remembering.

Being on the right path is remembering the power of love because love is important when dealing with emotions that can be carried around within your heart. Remembering that you are here for important spiritual lessons and the growth of love within your spirit will help you in your day-to-day life.

Know that you are on the right spiritual path while you keep love in your heart at all times.

April 16

You must specifically ask for an Angel.

It is important to remember that Angels cannot just come into your life when you need help. You must specifically ask for their help. It is also important to be grateful and say thank you for their divine wisdom, love, help, and support in your life because being grateful raises your vibrational frequency.

Ask an Angel for help and remember to say thank you to them. Write down how they have helped or guided you.

April 17

Failure is not an option.

People that succeed in life never give up and never stop trying until they reach their goal—failure is never an option. Success often does not come easy and does require hard work. Most overnight successes have been from people manifesting and working hard towards their goals and dreams for many years. Failure is not something to be feared because you can never fail. Everything you do, no matter whether you view it as a success or failure holds a valuable spiritual lesson for you. By looking at a perceived failure as a valuable lesson, it no longer feels challenging and becomes a success.

Today, dig your heels in and keep trying to achieve your goals. You will succeed in some way if you don't give up. Write down all your successes today no matter how big or how small.

April 18

Karma teaches you to live in peace.

Positive and negative karma refers to actual positive or negative actions. It also refers to an intent or motive. For example, even if you do the smallest daily action or deed with great love in your hearts, you can change your life from one of constantly creating negative karma to one of constantly creating good karma.

Understand that it is important to live your life in peace and harmony in order to complete your spiritual lessons and this is done, in part, through your karma.

A DAY IN SPIRIT

April

April 19

Angels are centered within the heart of the Divine.

Angels are centered within the heart of the Divine. They are in God's presence and grace at all times. An Angel is created to serve, love, hold, and guide those to whom they are assigned and those who ask for angelic support. Angels can be found in every corner of the Universe and are countless in numbers. If you could see Angels with the naked eye, you would be amazed at just how populated the Earth really is.

Look around and realize that there are many amazing and wonderful beings here, helping Earth and the people on it, even though they may not be visible for all to see.

April 20

Find peace within.

What makes you peaceful? What obstacles in life have either blocked your peace or, on the other hand, brought you to peace? Remember, peace starts from within, so it is important to keep this emotion in your heart at all times when determining your spiritual lessons.

Today, find things in your life that bring you peace from within and write them down.

April 21

Cultivate compassion.

As human beings you have the potential to be happy and cultivate compassionate or be harmful to others. The Dalai Lama says, "Thus we can strive gradually to become more compassionate, that is, we can develop both genuine sympathy for others' suffering and the will to help remove their pain. As a result, our own serenity and inner strength will increase." Thus, it is when you reach out to others who are suffering in some way; you are practicing compassion and following the Dalai Lama's advice while simultaneously finding greater peace within your own life.

Ask yourself, are you living your life with compassion? Write down how can you become more compassionate?

April 22

Live consciously.

You are made of energy composed of your thoughts, words, actions, feelings, a physical element, and spirit. You can live consciously to create illumination, joy, healing, hope, balance, harmony, courage, strength, love, wisdom, and power from within your soul and your spirit by being aware of your every thought and action and its effect on all that is.

Try and think about your thoughts, actions, and words today and how it affects others. Write down one way you can live consciously.

April 23

Remember your soul's purpose.

Your physical body is a temporary vessel where you choose to house your soul for a short span of time in the realms of material expression. Because of this, your soul has a record of all that it has experienced throughout many ages and lifetimes called the Akashic Records. Accessing these records through meditation can help you remember the lessons you are working on and your soul's purpose while here on Earth.

Ask yourself what is your soul putting in your Akashic Record in this life? Write down three good things that are being written.

April 24

Live life in forgiveness.

Forgiveness is living in a state of grace, and you are only truly happy when you forgive everyone in your life. Living in forgiveness is one of the most difficult spiritual lessons because it requires tremendous amounts of strength. It takes a lot of energy to hold onto hatred or disrespect to others but when you live in forgiveness, you can affect your karma in a positive way by being in the light of all of human consciousness.

Try to forgive someone who has hurt you deeply today. Write down why you can forgive them.

April 25

Love is all we need.

By keeping love in your hearts at all times, it will make it easier to change your energy or vibrational frequency because your words, actions, and thoughts make up this energy. Living in loving tolerance for all living and non–living things on Earth will help you keep your heart chakras open and ascend to higher dimensional consciousness.

Who in your life needs love and understanding today?

April 26

Give to others and give to the earth.

When picking up trash from the street and recycling it, you are in service to the earth. When you listen to others and give them kind words, thoughts, and actions, you are in service to humanity and, therefore, the earth because your vibrational frequency affects everything around you. Living a life in service to others and to your environment is a good way to change your energy and dissipate any challenging karma you have brought forth from a past life and to create new and better karma for yourself in your current life and future lives.

Remember, giving or being in service helps raise your vibrational frequency and affects your karma in positive ways. How are you giving to others and the earth?

April 27

Be grateful.

Gratitude is the fastest way to raise your vibrational frequency. Start each morning by placing one foot on the floor and saying, "Thank" and with the other foot say, "You." The words, "Thank you" are great words of gratitude. You should be grateful for both positive and negative experiences in your life, for you have spiritual lessons in both.

What is one positive and one negative thing you are grateful for today?

A DAY IN SPIRIT

April 28

Be kind to yourself, others, and the earth.

You are all connected. When you hurt yourself, others, and the earth, you create a negative web of energy around the planet, which makes it harder for you to ascend to higher dimensional consciousness. Through kindness to all things in life, the negative web can be broken and ascension for all can be possible.

Say a kind word to someone today or do something kind for the Earth. Write down what this is.

April 29

Don't judge others; you don't know what their life's purpose is.

You don't know what the Angels have planned for another soul. As each and every person is in the various stages of progression in life, you must remember not to judge others. If you hold kindness in your hearts for all, you can walk as if you are Angels on Earth as you strive towards spiritual perfection.

Walk as if you are an Angel on Earth today. How does this make you feel?

April 30

Be happy and be at peace.

If you are not happy, then you will be unable to share happiness and peacefulness with others. You all have a light within and should take every opportunity to shine and hold that light not only on yourself, but on all of humanity.

Think about what makes you both happy and at peace today.

A DAY IN SPIRIT

MAY

May 1

Identify with spiritual strength.

Don't identify with emotions—identify with spiritual strength. Adverse circumstances should not dictate your visions of yourself. Physical and mental hardships have to do with self-definition, but it is your spirit that actually defines who you are and what greatness you are capable of. Great power and strength does not lie with great intellect or physical prowess, it lies with spiritual strength.

Realize that great power and strength lie within your spirit. Write down three spiritual strengths that make you who you are.

May 2

What you dwell upon, you create.

When you have pressing issues in your life, you put your energy into eliminating these issues that seem to come back over and over again. These scenarios might include people, situations, or specific problems that just won't go away. If you stop fighting them, thinking about them, and worrying about them, your worries will manifest in a more positive way. Again, what you dwell upon, you create, so it's always good to dwell upon and create positive circumstances and positive interactions.

Today, make your thoughts about positive circumstances and situations.

May 3

The Law of Attraction states that like attracts like.

Everything around you is energy; everything in the Universe is made up of tiny molecules that vibrate at a specific frequency. The Law of Attraction states that like attracts like. The law works universally on every plane of action, and you will always attract whatever you desire or expect. Determine resolutely to expect only what you desire, then you will attract only what you wish for.

Look at your friends and think about how their energy matches your energy. Write down how you are like your friends or vice versa.

May 4

Your Angels are everywhere, there is no limit.

Angels are everywhere, and you can ask for Angels to assist you with anything you wish that is for your higher purpose or higher good. There is no limit to the number of Angels you can ask for. There is an Angel available for any particular task, and they come to you as an answer to your wishes and prayers. You are able to order an Angel in order to request anything you want, need, wish, or desire.

You don't need a prayer to call an Angel to your side. Today, simply think, "Angels, please surround me, help me, protect me, and guide me" and they will be there.

May 5

Live your life in abundance.

Living in abundance isn't only about good energy flow and manifesting; it is also about staying in a positive frame of mind. When creating or manifesting with Angels and Guides, it is important to be happy in the current moment without needing a reason for this happiness. Being happy without needing a reason to be happy is the ultimate freedom and releases you from outside influences. You are always free from having other people control you when you are happy and able to live your life in peace, happiness, and joy without restrictions.

Ask yourself if you are staying positive during your day.

May 6

See the great compassion you hold within your heart.

Great compassion lies within each and every heart. Compassion is a feeling deep within yourself, a "quivering of the heart," and it is also a way of acting—being affected by the suffering of others and moving on their behalf. The practice of compassion increases your capacity to care. It also reinforces charity, empathy, and sympathy.

Today, practice compassion. Write down how you are doing that.

May 7

Meditate every day.

Meditating will allow you to create your own healthy and peaceful life. Meditation brings physical and mental calmness and enhances the power of concentration, memory, intuition, inner strength, and peace of mind. The ultimate goal of meditation is to reach beyond the mind and live in the world of pure spirit. If you meditate, and persevere with earnestness and concentration, you will eventually come to realize that there is a world beyond thoughts. You will be able to silence your thoughts, and then meditation will take a new meaning. You will discover the joy and bliss that comes when the mind is silent. You will discover a new kind of consciousness, which is beyond the mind and is not dependent on it.

Practice meditating to a state of consciousness where you have no thoughts.

May 8

Live your life in awareness.

Awareness is a term referring to your ability to perceive, to feel or to be conscious of events, objects, or patterns. Spiritual awareness or spiritual awakening is the process by which you begin to explore your own being and your own spirit in order to become whole and reunite with your true spiritual meaning.

Ask yourself, what can you be more aware of today?

May 9

Karma teaches you to live your life with love.

You should live your life in love of others and for others without any expectation of repayment. You should live your life in love, forgiving hurts against you, asking for the consolation of dead relatives and friends, and loving everyone with no distinction between friend and foe. This brings about true lasting joy and happiness, good karma, and virtue to yourselves, your loved ones, and the world. If you are kind to others, even those who are not kind to you, you will find true happiness.

Today, begin to live your life with love. Write down steps to help you achieve this goal.

A DAY IN SPIRIT

May 10

Shift your consciousness.

By shifting your consciousness and connecting to humanity, you can be more conscious of what you are doing to yourself and how you need to change your community life in order to create a more nourishing, peaceful, and loving situations that will foster your continued spiritual growth.

Ask yourself, what do you want to help change today?

May 11

You have come to this planet to grow and learn your spiritual lessons.

You have come to this planet to grow and learn your spiritual lessons. But you have also come with a specific purpose—to help the planet with its spiritual evolution by raising your energy and consciousness and by connecting to each other.

If there are spiritual lessons each day of your life, what are these lessons?

May 12

Messages you are receiving at this time from the Universe are messages of the heart.

Messages you are receiving at this time from the Universe are messages of the heart. As a group you are working to help humanity open its collective heart chakra and embrace higher energy and higher consciousness. You are also creating a new society based on love and empowerment. It is a society that exists beyond duality in the realm of oneness.

Analyze a thought or even a feeling you have today that may be a message from the Universe. Write this thought or feeling down.

May 13

Change is possible within each of us.

You can overcome conflict and hatred, spanning seemingly timeless generations, and live in peace. You can grow and rise above limitations in stagnant and outdated non–spiritual beliefs and policies that hurt your world as a whole. This change starts within you.

What small thing can you change in your life today?

May 14

Live your life as an Angel.

When an argument arises, you can step back and look at everyone concerned and ask, "How would an Angel or Guide react?" An Angel or Guide would react with gentleness, forgiveness, and love. Not with anger, hate, or spite. You must see the higher view and ask, "Is this argument really important? Is there another way to deal with this issue?" When you lash out in anger, your spiritual lessons and advancement are lost.

Today, walk as if you are an Angel on Earth by rising above confrontation and seeing the true spiritual meaning of all that is.

May 15

Remember your karma.

Karma is also important when connecting to humanity. Every thought you have, every word that you speak either adds to or takes away from the light of humanity. Everything you think and say about yourself, whether it is silently to yourself or aloud to others, either adds to or takes away from the light of humanity. Everything you think and say to and about others, whether it is silently to yourself or aloud to others, either adds to or takes away from the light of humanity. There are no insignificant thoughts or words; each one has energy and an effect.

Today, ask yourself how your thoughts, words, and actions affect others and vice versa. This will help you remember your karma.

May 16

Forgiveness is the foundation of all spiritual work.

Forgiveness is the foundation of all spiritual work and growth because it is through awareness that you can truly know your own life's journey and perspective. Forgiveness is not a process of giving something to another person, who may not deserve anything, but it is instead a process of turning your energy inward and using the power of love to look closely at your relationships with others and yourself.

Remember, when anchored in forgiveness, you are within the spiritual realm of conscious awareness rather than in the realm of emotions or the mind.

May 17

An "eye for an eye" will leave everyone blind.

The Dalai Lama once said that, "An eye for an eye will leave everyone blind." You must be careful not to judge others and to be kind to all, even people who are not kind to you, and you will truly be happy. If you stay connected to humanity through your compassionate spirits, anything can be possible in your life and on Earth. Death, punishment, and cruelty are not the way to change humanity, living in the light is.

Think about how peace is the way for all aspects in your life. Write down how you can be more peaceful to others.

May 18

You will always have hope.

If there is one thing you have always had and will always have, and that is hope. Hope is the most incredible word. This word not only means to wish for something but to wait with expectation for its fulfillment. It is an emotional belief in a positive outcome related to events and circumstances within one's personal life. It is a belief that there will be a positive outcome even when there is evidence to the contrary.

What does hope mean to you and what do you hope for in your life and the lives of others?

A DAY IN SPIRIT

May 19
Everything in life is related.

Native American writings and most religions that are based on earth–centered philosophies say you are all related in life. If you treat yourself with love, respect, and compassion, you will have that same love, respect, and compassion for all things on Earth and in life. You are all part of the same whole; you are all rowing the same boat, so to speak. Your souls have the capability to find a way to allow your spirits to shine with great light and intensity by just being who you are and understanding that you are here for a reason.

Today, understand that if you hurt others or the environment, you are only hurting yourself. Write down one way you think you are related to this Earth and the people on it.

May 20
The Universe is composed of energy.

The energy of the Universe flows among, between, and within everything around you. When you have internal blocks, your energy fails to flow correctly within your meridians. This causes illness, disease, and other symptoms in your body. When your meridians flow freely, your energy promotes health, prevents disease, and cures illness. This energy can be directed consciously in a manner in which you can see and feel.

Today, think about your energy and what you can do to make it better.

May 21
You are beings of both spirit and human nature.

You are spiritual beings, but at the same time, you are souls living on Earth. You inhabit both worlds simultaneously even though you are often unaware of it. You should embrace both your physical and spiritual realm as both are equally important. You have to walk with one foot in each of these worlds with the understanding that they go hand–in–hand with the cycles of reincarnation and karma. Neglecting either your spiritual or earthly side can cause distress and misunderstanding of your true purpose. Remembering that you have agreed to come here from the spiritual realm can help you stay focused on mastering your spiritual lessons.

Today, ask yourself why do you think your spirit is here on this Earth and what your purpose is?

May 22

No one soul is superior to another.

No one being or creature is any better or of more importance than another—you are all the same. You are all in various stages of your spiritual evolution and have different levels of understanding. This does not make any one person better than another, and you should never judge others as you are unaware of their lessons. You are not masters of nature, plants, or animals. They are your companions and co–inhabitants of your planet. You are not superior to any other living thing nor do you own them. You are simply the caregivers of this planet and should treat everyone and everything with love, understanding, compassion, and respect.

What can you do today to show your Angels and Guides that you are living life with love and compassion of all living things?

May 23

Belief creates.

What you dwell on, you create. And you have the ability to manifest anything you want or need if you simply believe in it. Think about what you plan to manifest—then use your imagination to feel this within your spirit. You can feel happy, successful, strong, or anything else you desire. Then, remain confident while your manifestations come to fruition.

What incredibly and wondrous things do you believe in today?

May 24

Trust your intuition.

Inside of you, a voice speaks and guides you. This is your intuition, and it is often guided by your higher self, Angels, and Guides. You can choose to ignore your intuition or you can choose to listen to it. However, once you are in tune with your intuition and start listening to it, you will be guided and will find that any goal is achievable in your life. When you realize that Spirit works through you, it will be to your benefit. Remember, your Angels, Guides, and higher self will always help guide you in your life when asked and are always working for your highest good.

What is the last thing you remember that you felt you were somehow guided and helped by some higher form?

May 25

Karma is impersonal.

Karma operates on universal laws, which create total justice. Karma is very impersonal, and it applies to everyone at all times—without exception. Karma makes you realize that you are all interrelated, irrespective of our nationality, religion, race, creed, sex, etc.; and thereby teaches you the Law of One—that you are all connected to each other. Karma also teaches you to take ownership of yourself as it makes you responsible for your actions in all aspects of your life. Remember, karma gives you an understanding of the cause and effect of your thoughts and actions, so make these thoughts and actions positive.

What can you do to create positive karma for yourself?

May 26

There is a higher purpose.

Everything that happens in your life happens for a reason and for your greater good. You have to learn to look at events in your life from more than just a normal human perspective. You must see these events from an elevated spiritual platform and look at what spiritual lessons and spiritual growth will come from these events. All is as it should be in life. There is no such thing as accidents. Everything is in compliance with Divine timing.

Today, think about how good and challenging things that are happening in your life are for a specific or higher purpose?

May 27

There are no ordinary moments.

The past only exists as your memory, and the future only exists as your expectation. The only moment in time that counts is now, this moment. Every moment in life is precious, and you should treat it as such and live each moment to the fullest because by being in the present, you have presence. To live in the now, the conscious mind should be quiet and focused on what you are doing, not what you are doing next week or what happened yesterday. The past is no longer there; the future is not here yet.

Remember, there is only one moment in which life is meant to be lived, and that is the present moment. Live today in this present moment.

A DAY IN SPIRIT

May 28

There are no limits.

The only limits you have are those you place upon yourself or others place upon you, and to this end, you should avoid being limited by others. If someone views a dog as being aggressive, then it is more likely to be aggressive. Holding expectations of others and limiting them, stunts their spiritual growth. What you think about you manifest, and what you visualize you create. If you make your manifestations and creations positive and enlightening, then life will be without limitations and your souls can soar.

Ask yourself how are you limiting things in your life and how can you change this to being limitless.

May 29

Action not reaction is important.

If you are tickled, your reaction is to laugh. Living in a state of awareness where you do not react in any given situation, but act instead reflects a life living in consciousness. Reaction is unconscious whereas action is conscious, and you should not let past influences affect your current actions. There are times to act, as well as times to be still. By living in the present moment and having control of your conscious mind, you can better direct your actions and, therefore, your life.

Try and spend this day living in the present moment with action and not reaction. How are you doing this?

May 30

Positivity rules.

Negative thoughts attract negative actions, situations, and people and can create challenging karma. Positive thoughts attract positive actions, situations, and people and can create good karma. You should look at your thoughts and the events that happen to you in a positive light, recognizing negative thoughts for what they are, and releasing them to the Universe. By remaining positive and seeing the good in all people and all situations, you can create a reality where a light will always shine upon you.

Today, stay positive and see how this positivity changes your life. Write down one positive thing you did today.

May 31

Posture, pose, and breathing help maintain life.

Energy flows through your bodies as it flows through all things in life. If your posture and pose are incorrect, your energy cannot flow clearly; this creates blockages that can manifest as pain or illness. You breathe in energy from the world around you; therefore, your breaths should be deep and full, coming from the bottom of the belly and not the chest. This enables you to maximize your energy and helps you to relax. When you are stressed, angry, or afraid, your breathing changes and becomes shallow and fast. By consciously controlling your breathing and keeping it deep and even, you can release stress, anger, or fear, so you can act consciously from an elevated platform in whatever situation you are in.

Today, stand or sit up tall, breathe deeply, and feel your energy get better.

MAY

A DAY IN SPIRIT

JUNE

June 1

Hearing and seeing is believing.

Everyone is born with spiritual gifts, but most aren't aware that they have them or how to develop them. Angels and guides will try many times to reach you in your lives. They are here to help and guide you and you should always trust that inner feeling you have when you feel as if you are being helped. Know that you are loved, never alone, and always being helped from behind the scenes in life.

Often in life we say, "When you see it, you will believe it." Today, try and say, "When I believe it, I will see it."

June 2

You can change the world.

Every single person on this Earth is important. You are that one person and what you think, say, and do matters and makes a difference. Be the change you wish to see on this planet by making a difference. There are no insignificant thoughts, words, or actions and each one is an effect on the world around you.

Make everything you do today count towards making the world a better place. You can change the world with only one action.

June 3

Change happens.

Change is continuous and is always happening around you. You cannot always perceive change, but you can see the end result of it. Change is not a negative thing, nor should it be feared. Through change you can grow and move forward in your life, learning your spiritual lessons along the way. If you chose not to change, you will become stagnant in your spiritual growth and, therefore, your spiritual evolution.

Think about what you need to change in your life today and make that change.

June 4
Take responsibility for your actions.

Actions can cause reactions. It is the Law of Cause and Effect. For every action there is an equal and opposite reaction, including a karmic boomerang. You have to be aware of your actions, take responsibility for them, and be conscious of their consequences. When being critical, judgmental or unsupportive of others, you are lowering your vibrational frequency and creating challenging karma. By taking responsibility for your own actions, you can take back the power of your spirit and the freedom to choose good thoughts, words and actions, which in turn create good karma.

Today, take responsibility of your actions and make them positive. Write down one change you can make.

June 5
Clean out your clutter physically, emotionally, and spiritually.

Cleaning out clutter allows you to open a door to the Universe and make room for more goodness to come into your life. By cleaning out clutter, you are making a path for new experiences, new opportunities, and new energy to come into your life.

Today, clean out a drawer, closet, or room and release any negative emotional energy to the Universe.

June 6
Never sit in judgment.

You have no right to judge others for their words, thoughts, or actions because you don't know what their spiritual lessons are. You have the freedom of choice to do as you please and act as you wish, and it is up to you to live your life in consciousness or unconsciousness. You are in no position to judge anyone, as you are imperfect souls striving in your spiritual evolution, and by judging others, you lower your vibrational frequency. Everyone has a life's purpose and you don't know what that life purpose is or what spiritual lessons that you, your Guides or your Angels have pre-planned for yourself or others.

Who have you been judging and how can you change that negative energy into understanding and positive energy?

June 7

Act with integrity.

Integrity is how you act when no one else is looking—it is the concept of consistency of actions, values, and principles. You must live by your own standards and should not judge others by these standards. Your life is about living in conjunction with your highest spiritual intentions, experience, and lessons and nothing else. Being kind, living your life with integrity, and always doing the right thing is spiritually rewarded and helps you with your spiritual progression.

Ask yourself if you do the right thing when no–one is watching?

June 8

You have a "Guardian Angel" with you in life.

Another type of Angel with you during your life is your Guardian Angel. A Guardian Angel is an angelic being that is dedicated to serve and to help you throughout your lifetime. However, the relationship is somewhat deeper than that. Your Guardian Angel was created out of the same essence that makes up your soul. It could be said to be a higher or essence aspect of yourself. Guardian Angels are also called tutelary Angels because they stay with you, watching over your life, protecting you, and encouraging your spiritual well–being and happiness.

Meditate and connect with your Guardian Angel today. They are with you always—helping you, guiding you, and loving you. Write down any messages you receive.

June 9

Life is an ongoing journey.

Your journeys and explorations through life never stop. In truth, they continue for many lifetimes. The destination is not the reward or the goal in your spiritual evolution; it is the journey to the destination that is the goal itself. The spiritual lessons learned are always your rewards, and you should not forget that your Angels and Guides want you to have fun in all your journeys along your life's path.

Remember, your Angels and Guides want you to have fun in your journey in life. Write down three positive experiences in your life's journey.

A DAY IN SPIRIT

June 10

Change your mind.

If you take an objective view of your mind, then you can see that many thoughts drift through it, many of which you are unaware. A sad, angry, or fearful thought may drift up from the sub–conscious and change how you feel for no apparent reason. If you take control of your mind through tools such as meditation and become aware of these thoughts, you can realize them for what they are. Then you can release any negative thoughts to the Universe, while remaining relaxed, calm, and centered.

Today, consciously focus your mind and release negative energy and change your minds from negative thought patterns to positive thought patterns.

June 11

Emotions come and go.

Emotions flow through you at all times, often without you realizing it. Many of you do not express your emotions because you feel you have to act or behave in a specific manner. When you feel negative emotions, you can feel your bodies become tense; if you do not express these emotions when you feel them, the tension is stored within your bodies, energy, and aura. Having emotions should not be feared but should be celebrated. When you feel an emotion, you should express it. If you are happy, you should smile and laugh, and if you are sad you should cry. Expressing your emotions releases tension and helps you live more fully in the current moment.

Today, express your emotions in a positive way.

June 12

Don't forget to play and laugh.

Playing is one of our greatest joys and sources of pleasure in life. It takes many forms, from sports to games to laughing and joking with friends. Playing increases your energy and keeps you in a positive frame of mind. It makes those around you more positive and generally lifts the spirits of all involved. There are times to be serious, yes, but there are times to play, too, and that is what you must remember.

Today, laugh and play as much as possible. Write down how this makes you feel.

June 13

Have good thoughts and actions each day.

Your character is dependent on good thoughts, actions, and words. When you have thoughts, these have an effect on your circumstances and, therefore, your karma. For example, if you hit someone, you may cause harm, pain, or injury to the person and the law of karma requires you to experience the same pain. This happens so you learn to behave in a way that causes good experiences to others and especially to yourself. Instead, have good thoughts and actions and see how your energy changes.

Today, continue to have both good thoughts and actions and your life will continue to change for the better.

June 14

The law of karma affects all that is.

The law of karma affects all that is, including friends, families, cities, and even countries. It also affects all that you do toward anyone or anything—including humans, animals, plants, trees, and beings of any nature. Every action, thought, and emotion is energy and this radiates into the Universe like a radio station.

Today, ask yourself what good things are happening to you through your positive outlook?

June 15

Your energy ripples through the Universe.

All your energy is constantly rippling through the Universe. Your thoughts and emotions, no matter how private you may consider them, affect others around you. You are a result of the energy you create from your thoughts and actions, which, again, contributes to your karmic balance sheet. This energy is also part of your aura and affects everything around you, including your family, friends, the world, and even the Universe.

Today, ask yourself if the energy you put out to the Universe is positive?

June 16

Angels are everywhere and you can ask for Angels to assist you with anything you wish.

By asking Angels to be present everywhere in your life, you will begin to embody angelic qualities. You will be more open to the love and abundance of the Universe. You will begin to experience more joy, health, and laughter as you sense the wings of Angels flying around every aspect of your life. Ask for their help and then feel their beautiful presence by your side.

Your spiritual connection with your Angels if very real. Believe, trust, and have faith in this connection.

June 17

Karma is not fate.

Fate is a notion of predestination. Karma is specifically chosen with the purpose of undergoing a learning experience. This means you may find yourself pulled to people or situations for a reason. Because of free will and various types of karma, your paths can be altered while you are living here on Earth. You will have many chances to learn your spiritual lessons since opportunities are presented to you on a regular basis.

Today, remember the more you are aware, grow, and learn from your spiritual lessons, the more your life can be altered for the better.

June 18

Great karmic strides can be made with intention.

Intention is the most important of all mental processes because it guides the mind in determining how to engage with virtuous, non–virtuous, or neutral objects. Just as iron is powerlessly drawn to a magnet, your mind is drawn to the object of your intentions. An intention is a mental thought or action that may be expressed through either a physical or a verbal action.

Today, work on your intention because what you dwell on with intention, you manifest.

A DAY IN SPIRIT

June 19

Begin at this moment to have a happier life.

Living in the present moment will allow you to manifest happiness flowing into your life. See it, feel it, think it, and breathe it into your being. You will change your energy by being happier and living in the present moment.

Do something today that makes you happy and keeps you in your present moment.

June 20

Forgiveness is a strong foundation.

When you are anchored in forgiveness, you are within the spiritual realm rather than in the realm of emotions or the mind. How often do you forgive others while still holding on to that corner of your heart that says, "I am right and they are wrong, but I forgive them?" By forgiving others, you will find true happiness and also free up energy in your heart.

Forgive someone today that you wouldn't normally forgive and release that energy from your heart. Write down how that makes you feel.

June 21

Love is the healing energy that binds all of humanity.

By tying up your spiritual energy reserves into old issues, you are limiting the vibrational level of love available in your present life. Now is the time to begin searching your hearts to find out how to truly forgive. Once you do it once or twice, you will find love is what connects us all beneath all hurt and pain.

Try to keep love in your heart as you walk your spiritual path today.

June 22

Don't judge.

You don't know others' spiritual lessons or their spiritual evolutionary paths, so you must never judge anyone because it lowers your vibrational frequency and leaves you without compassion. Keeping compassion in your hearts for all living and non–living things is important since compassion is yet another powerful emotion that heals.

Today, understand you are a spiritual being on a human journey and must keep yourself from lowering your vibrational frequency through being judgmental.

June 23

Let go of the past.

One of the hardest things to do in life is to let go of the past. Dwelling on issues for too long can close your heart chakras and keep you from being fully present in your current moment. When you are not fully present in the now, you are not living your life to the fullest, you are not free and your energy fields get tied up running old programs, blocking you from receiving love and knowledge from the Universe.

Today, truly let go of something that is bothering you and release those past worries into the Universe.

June 24

Embark on a path of self-discovery, self-healing, and spiritual growth.

Your decision to embark on a path of self–discovery, self–healing, and spiritual growth is one that requires great courage, perseverance, and determination. You are a soul that is strong enough and wise enough to discover and walk this path.

Today, realize you are a brave and strong soul that can make it through this life with great success no matter what obstacles lay before you.

June 25

Search for joy and love each and every day.

While on Earth, you must learn to cope with intolerance, anger, and sadness while searching for joy and love. Along the way you must not lose your integrity, sacrifice goodness for survival, or acquire superior or inferior attitudes to those around you. You know that living in an imperfect world will help you to appreciate the true meaning of perfection.

Today, experience joy and love deep within your hearts and share this love and joy with others.

June 26

Your spirit never dies.

The greatest gift of living a life in awareness is knowing that your spirit never dies. You have absolute freedom to experience everything that life has to offer in all of its full glory. It is said that it is not the destination in life but the journey that makes you who you are. The trip itself is not about knowing but about experiencing.

Today, understand that your spirit and the experiences you encounter are your only purpose; they are what life is.

June 27

Be aware.

You are all sitting on a spiritual gold mine, filled with enriched experiences that can make life much happier and meaningful if you are more aware and conscious of these experiences. You note some of your spiritual experiences in your life, but many more are missed. This is why many of your life's lessons are lost—because you lack awareness of what truly is.

Be aware of all your spiritual experiences every day of your life starting today. Write one of these down.

A DAY IN SPIRIT

June 28
Find peace within.

What makes you peaceful? What obstacles in life have either blocked your peace or, on the other hand, brought you to peace? Remember, peace starts from within, so it is important to keep this emotion in your heart at all times when living day to day and determining a spiritual lesson.

Today, discover what experiences in your heart and in your life bring you peace.

June 29
Cultivate compassion.

Are you living your life with compassion? As human beings you all have the potential to be both happy and compassionate people or miserable and harmful to others. The Dalai Lama says, "Thus we can strive gradually to become more compassionate, that is, we can develop both genuine sympathy for others' suffering and the will to help remove their pain. As a result, our own serenity and inner strength will increase." Thus, it is when you reach out to others who are suffering in some way; you are practicing compassion while simultaneously finding greater peace within your own life.

Each and every day strive to cultivate compassion for others within your beautiful soul.

June 30
Live consciously.

You are made of energy composed of your thoughts, words, actions, feelings, a physical element, and your spirit. You can live consciously to create illumination, joy, healing, hope, balance, harmony, courage, strength, love, wisdom, and power from within your soul and your spirit by being aware and conscious of your every thought and action and its effect on all that is.

Today, open your eyes, minds, and hearts to the true meaning of the experiences you will live today and be conscious of these experiences.

A DAY IN SPIRIT

JULY

July 1

Remember your soul's purpose.

Your physical body is a temporary vessel where you choose to house your soul for a short span of time in the realms of material expression. Because of this, your soul has a record of all that it has experienced throughout many ages and lifetimes called the Akashic Records. Accessing these records through meditation can help you remember the lessons you are working on and your soul's purpose.

Ask yourself, "Why am I here. What do I need to learn today?"

July 2

Everything in life is related.

Native American writings and most religions that are based on earth–centered philosophies say you are all related in life. If you treat yourself with love, respect and compassion, you will have that same love, respect and compassion for all things on Earth and in life. You are all part of the same whole; you are all rowing the same boat, so to speak. Your souls have the capability to find a way to allow your spirits to shine with great light and intensity by just being who you are and understanding that you are here for a reason.

Today, have respect and compassion for all people in all walks of life.

July 3

The Universe is composed of energy.

The energy of the Universe flows among, between, and within everything around you. When you have internal blocks, your energy fails to flow correctly within your meridians. This causes illness, disease, and other symptoms in your bodies. When your meridians flow freely, your energy promotes health, prevents disease, and cures illness. This energy, or chi, can be directed consciously in a manner in which you can see and feel. Your thoughts, words, and actions make up your aura or energy field and what you think, say, and do affect this aura or energy field.

Today, understand that negative actions and thoughts can drain energy while positive actions and thoughts can create good energy.

July 4
You are beings of both spirit and human nature.

You are spiritual beings, but at the same time, you are souls living on Earth. You inhabit both worlds simultaneously even though you are often unaware of it. You should embrace both your physical and spiritual realm as both are equally important. You have to walk with one foot in each of these worlds with the understanding that they go hand-in-hand with the cycles of reincarnation and karma. Neglecting either your spiritual or earthly side can cause distress and misunderstanding of your true purpose.

Today, remember that you have agreed to come here from the spiritual realm and this can help you stay focused on mastering your spiritual lessons.

July 5
No one soul is superior to another.

No one being or creature is any better or of more importance than another—you are all the same. You are all in various stages of your spiritual evolution and have different levels of understanding. This does not make any one person better than another, and you should never judge others as you are unaware of their lessons. You are not masters of nature, plants, or animals. They are your companions and co–inhabitants of your planet.

Today, recognize that you are simply the caregivers of this planet and should treat everyone and everything with love, understanding, compassion, and respect.

July 6
Remember that you all share a common home, your planet and a common race, humanity.

Mahatma Gandhi once said that an "eye for an eye" would leave everybody blind. It is no secret that this planet has reached a global crisis; we are living among systems that no longer serve the good of humanity. Take a close look at the world around you; the world is becoming more impoverished. The rich are getting richer, and the poor are getting poorer and taken advantage of. Everyone is rowing the same boat so to speak in different ways and you must learn to live in loving tolerance of these differences.

How will you honor Earth and all living and non–living things on it today?

July 7
Trust your intuition.

Inside of you, a voice speaks and guides you. This is your intuition, and it is often guided by your higher self, Angels and Guides. You can choose to ignore your intuition or you can choose to listen to it. Once you are in tune with your intuition and start listening to it, you will be guided and will find that any goal is achievable in your life. When you realize that Spirit works through you, it will be to your benefit.

Remember, today that your Angels, Guides, and higher self will always help guide you in your life when asked and are always working for your highest good.

July 8
There is a higher purpose.

Everything that happens in your life happens for a reason and for your greater good. You have to learn to look at events in your life from more than just a normal human perspective. You must see these events from an elevated spiritual platform and look at what spiritual lessons and spiritual growth will come from both good and bad events in your life. All is as it should be in life.

Today, understand that there is no such thing as accidents—everything is in compliance with Divine timing. Write down what you think your higher purpose is.

July 9
There are no ordinary moments.

The past only exists as your memory, and the future only exists as your expectation. The only moment in time that counts is now, this moment. Every moment in life is precious, and you should treat it as such and live each moment to the fullest because by being in the present, you have presence. To live in the now, the conscious mind should be quiet and focused on what you are doing, not what you are doing next week or what happened yesterday. The past is no longer there; the future is not here yet.

Today, believe that there is only one moment in which life is meant to be lived, and that is the present moment.

A DAY IN SPIRIT

July 10
There are no limits.

Your life is filled with limitless possibilities through your own imagination and you can create the life you want and deserve filled with joy and happiness. You have no limits on what you can create, be, and accomplish.

Do not limit yourself in any way today.

July 11
Action not reaction is important.

If you are tickled, your reaction is to laugh. Living in a state of awareness where you do not react in any given situation, but act instead, reflects a life living in consciousness. Reaction is unconscious whereas action is conscious, and you should not let past influences affect your current actions. There are times to act, as well as times to be still. By living in the present moment and having control of your conscious mind, you can better direct your actions and, therefore, your life.

Today, try not to react to negative emotions or people in your life but, instead, take action to make things better in a more positive way.

July 12
Positivity rules.

Negative thoughts attract negative actions, situations, and people and can create negative karma. Positive thoughts attract positive actions, situations and people and can create positive karma. You should look at your thoughts and the events that happen to you in a positive light, recognize negative thoughts for what they are, and release them to the Universe.

Today, remain positive and see the good in all people and in all situations so you can create a reality where a light will always shine upon you.

July 13

Posture, pose, and breathing help maintain life.

Energy flows through your bodies as it flows through all things in life. If your posture and pose are incorrect, your energy cannot flow clearly; this creates blockages that can manifest as pain or illness. You breathe in energy from the world around you; therefore, your breaths should be deep and full, coming from the bottom of the belly and not the chest. This enables you to maximize your energy and will help you to relax. When you are stressed, angry, or afraid, your breathing changes and becomes shallow and fast. By consciously controlling your breathing and keeping it deep and even, you can release stress, anger or fear, so you can act consciously from an elevated platform in whatever situation you are in.

Today, stand tall and breathe deeply while you visualize positive circumstances in your life.

July 14

Keep everything in balance.

The Universe exists in a state of balance, as should you. You can do almost anything you wish, but should always do it in moderation—never in excess and always in consciousness of all living and non–living things in this world. Anything in excess can become addictive, which drains energy. Staying balanced in your life allows you to keep and maintain a higher vibrational frequency.

Take a look at your life today and try to figure out if anything is energetically unbalanced, then fix that imbalance. Write down how you are doing this.

July 15

Intent is action.

You can intend to do anything, and your intent is important. However, unless the intent is followed with action, the intent will not come to fruition. For example, you may intend to train for a 10K race but spend your time going out to a movie or dinner with friends. You have intention, but your actions do not confirm or create the intention; therefore, you must use actions to create or manifest what you want. If action turns knowledge into wisdom, then consciousness is intent with action.

Today, be mindful of something and put action into that thought so it is conscious and this consciousness will help raise your vibrational frequency.

July 16
Freedom of choice is free will.

You all have free will and can choose to do almost anything you wish. There is no situation in life where you do not have a choice. Sometimes it takes a great amount of courage and strength to make the right decisions in life. You have the courage of conviction and the power of spirit to make any decisions necessary to lead you on a good karmic path where you are mindful of your spiritual lessons.

Remember, that your thoughts, words, and actions have a positive and conscious influence on all that you do. How are you choosing your decisions today?

July 17
Change happens.

Change is continuous and is always happening around you. You cannot always perceive change, but you can see the end result of it. Change is not a bad thing, nor should it be feared. Through change you can grow and move forward in your life, learning your spiritual lessons along the way. If you chose not to change, you will become stagnant in your spiritual growth and, therefore, your spiritual development lessons and evolution.

Today, slowly allow change to happen in your life. Write down what these changes are.

July 18
Take responsibility for your actions.

Actions can cause reactions. It is the Law of Cause and Effect. For every action there is an equal and opposite reaction, including a karmic boomerang. You have to be aware of your actions, take responsibility for them, and be conscious of their consequences. When being critical, judgmental, or unsupportive of others, you are lowering your vibrational frequency and creating bad karma. By taking responsibility for your own actions, you can take back the power of your spirit and the freedom to choose good thoughts, words and actions, which in turn creates good karma.

Work on your thoughts, words, and actions today and make them a good and positive force of energy.

A DAY IN SPIRIT

July 19

One step at a time.

To achieve any goal in life, it should be broken down into a number of smaller steps. If you have many small successes, this can lead to larger successes. If you aim for large goals too quickly, you may fail. Remember that every journey begins with a single step, then a second and a third and as many steps required until you reach your destination. You should reward and praise yourself for all your successes, however big or small they are.

Remember, what you dwell on you create, so manifest many goals in life and achieve success one step at a time. Today, write down a few steps you will take to achieve a goal you want.

July 20

Never sit in judgment.

You have the freedom of choice to do as you please and act as you wish, and it is up to you to live your life either consciously or unconsciously. You are in no position to judge anyone, as you are an imperfect soul striving in your spiritual evolution, and by judging others, you lower your vibrational frequency. Everyone has a life's purpose and you don't know what that life purpose is or what spiritual lessons that you, your Guides or your Angels have pre-planned for yourself or others.

Today, do not judge one person, but understand that each soul has a different spiritual journey than yours and be accepting of others.

July 21

It is all about integrity.

When you live from your own spiritual integrity, you are constantly inspired and energized to respond to change that is happening in this world with truth and honesty. Integrity means that your actions are in alignment with your heart all times and you are living a life of wholeness and openness while being an honest and good person each and every day.

Today, think about what you do today when nobody else is watching. Are you living a life for your highest good?

July 22

Change your thoughts and change your life.

The nature of your thoughts determines the quality of your life whether it is happy, sad, or contented. Happy, optimistic, positive thoughts, emotions, and feelings generate positive energy in your system which makes the blood flow freely and the heart beat joyously. These thoughts create a higher vibrational frequency and allows for better energy to enter your life.

Today, try changing your thoughts and the way you perceive yourself and the world around you as successful, then failure will not be an option.

July 23

Life is an ongoing journey.

Your journeys and explorations through life never stop. In truth, they continue for many lifetimes. The destination is not the reward or the goal in your spiritual evolution; it is the journey to the destination that is the goal itself. The spiritual lessons learned are always your rewards, and you should not forget that your Angels and Guides want you to have fun in all your journeys along your life's path.

Today, understand that life is an ongoing journey but you need to have fun while not hurting others, the environment or most importantly, yourself.

July 24

Don't stress.

Stress is a response to any situation or factor that creates a negative emotional or physical change or combination of both emotional and physical changes. Stress in an unavoidable aspect of life. People of all ages can experience stress and any excessive stress can interfere with life, activities, health, and energy. There should be nothing to stress about in life, as everything is in Divine timing with the Universe.

Today, release and let go of anything that is causing you stress.

July 25

Be a teacher of consciousness.

You are a teacher of consciousness because you see the smarter, brighter, and wiser way of bringing about change to our outdated systems we are living in. You are a soul on a newer energy grid that is filled with passion, focus, and honesty. You contain every tool necessary within your spirit to help others see a newer and better way of doing things with government, healthcare, and schools. Teach others to be aware. Teach others to live peacefully. Teach others to live their lives in consciousness.

Be a trailblazer to instigate change and show others the way of love and peace.

July 26

Create positive affirmations.

Affirmations impact the neurological functioning of the brain. Positive affirmations are like mantras. They have a sacred and spiritual force about them. Creating positive affirmations in your life will help you to manifest your dreams and wishes because what you dwell on you create.

Today, create a positive mantra that will help you manifest something positive in your life.

July 27

The purpose of karma is to maintain balance in the Universe.

In order for karmic balance to be maintained, living beings must learn their spiritual lessons and learn to live consciously and responsibly with an open mind that extends beyond just you. An open mind begins the path to enlightenment, and enlightenment brings greater understanding of all living and non–living things around you.

Today, be the walking miracle that you are. The miracle is not to fly in the air or walk on water, the miracle is to walk on Earth with a higher spiritual consciousness of all that walk with you.

A DAY IN SPIRIT

July 28

Live your life's purpose.

Living your life's purpose is another way to ascend. Many of you often ask, "What is my life's purpose?" Your life's purpose can be learned by communicating with your Angels and Guides or by simply allowing your life to be divinely guided so it can unfold into what you are meant to do and who you are meant to be.

Today, ask yourself why you are here in this body living this life and what you can do to learn and advance with your spiritual lessons.

July 29

What is your big mission?

What is a big mission? A big mission is some significant event that all of you have for your life—something that has a major impact on humanity or Earth, either negative or positive, depending on your spiritual advancement, position, and influence in life. The big mission can be any one of an infinite number of things, but it is different for every one of you, and in some way it makes a huge and lasting impact in the world that you do not always realize at the moment it happens.

Today, write out things that you feel you must accomplish in life or things you want to help change and this will help you discover what your big mission is.

July 30

Be a teacher and healer for humanity.

For beings of higher consciousness, incarnating on planet Earth at this time is an adventure. It is a group project in which millions of lightworkers are arriving as teachers and healers for humanity.

Today, be a teacher by living your light and shining that light on all you come across.

July 31

Let forgiveness be the foundation of all your spiritual work and growth.

If you are able to allow forgiveness to sit within your hearts, then great beauty and opportunity are within everyone, even those with old scars and betrayals buried deep within them. Forgiveness is not a process of giving something to another person who may not deserve it but is, instead, a process of turning your energy inward and using the power of love to examine your relationships within yourself and others. When you are anchored in forgiveness, you are all within the spiritual realm of conscious awareness rather than in the realm of emotions or the mind.

Today, anchor your heart in forgiveness so you can have a good foundation for your soul's work. Write down how you are going to forgive someone today.

JULY

A DAY IN SPIRIT

AUGUST

August 1

Your thoughts can change your life.

Through positive thoughts you can manifest anything you want or need in your life. It isn't what you have, who you are, where you are, or even what you are doing that makes you happy or unhappy. It is your thoughts that create all this for yourself.

Today, create happy thoughts throughout the day. Write a few of these happy thoughts down.

August 2

What are your new experiences going to be?

You cannot change your past experiences. They are there to help you learn spiritual lesson and to help your soul grow. However, you can determine what your new experiences are going to be. You can make this new day what you want it to be and you can change tomorrow for your thoughts are the cause, conditions, and manifestations of your life.

Ask yourself what positive new experiences you will be creating in your life today.

August 3

Have faith.

Great teachers of the world, such as Buddha, derived strength and inspiration not from muscle or intellect but from faith. Buddha spoke a great language that went straight to people's hearts. You, as a civilization or humanity, are no different. These teachings connect you through your heart chakras and ask you to have faith.

Today, don't lose hope or faith. Remember even when the sun goes down, the stars always come out.

August 4

Be a beacon of light and spread your light.

You can be a light and spread your light by focusing your intention on what you want in life. When you focus on what others have, you are seeing your life from a point of lack. By focusing your energies on what you have, you bring the light into your life and, in return, can spread this light to others. Each of you is important and your energy is continuously manifested all around you. You can take this power and use it wisely, for each of you has come to spread the light to the world.

You can spread your light today in two ways. You can be the candle that omits the light or you can be the mirror that reflects the light.

August 5

Your thoughts, actions, and words release spiritual energy into the Universe.

Through your thoughts, actions, and words, you are releasing spiritual energy into the Universe and are, in turn, affected by influences or energies coming in to you from all directions. You are your own sender and receiver of your thoughts and actions. As you sow, so shall you reap so make all your thoughts, actions, and words positive.

What you think about is what makes you happy. Today, have happy thoughts. Make a log of your happy thoughts.

August 6

Do you feel like you are here for a reason?

For most of you, it can take up to half your lifetimes to wake up to the fact that you have a mission or a purpose while here on Earth. Feeling that something is coming or that you have some big mission to accomplish is quite common among those of you who are waking up and becoming aware of who you are and why you are here. For many of you, there is a constant underlying feeling or thought that you should be doing something bigger or more important with your life—that you have something special to contribute that is bigger than yourself.

Your life's path is revealed to you today by spiritual guideposts. Watch for them as they will mark your way and lead you to your soul's ultimate purpose.

August 7

Your soul is a beacon of light.

Be like the sun always giving, always shining, to everyone, in every direction all the time. Your soul is like a beacon of light that can change the world by just sharing that light with others. You also have a gift to share this light upon others.

Today, keep your feet on the ground but let your heart soar and shine like the beacon of light that you are.

August 8

Create positive energy in your life.

Being aware of all your thoughts and emotions, as well as all your words and actions, will help you to create positive energy in your life. You must be prepared to receive the kind of energy you radiate both physically and in your thoughts and minds. Thoughts of violence toward others may hurt people just as much as any physical violence and may come back as a karmic boomerang. Thoughts of love and good will towards others will bring you a good karmic boomerang. If you are kind to all, even those who are not kind to you, you will find true happiness.

Today, know that every positive thought propels you into the right direction in your life. What are those positive thoughts today?

August 9

Karma is all about universal balance.

What goes around comes around; you reap what you sow. Each moment of life gives you the opportunity to become more balanced, to create new good karma, and to take another step on the path toward self–mastery. Despite the fact that you cannot change the past, the future is yours to shape. There is comfort in knowing there's always another chance. It's important to be aware of who you are and understand why you are here because your thoughts, words, and actions put coins into either your good karma piggy bank or your bad karma piggy bank.

Implement the teaching of spirituality today by utilizing the principles where you practice positivity, balance, and living without judgment.

A DAY IN SPIRIT

August 10

Happiness is a spiritual experience.

Happiness cannot be owned, purchased, or consumed. Happiness is found by living through your heart chakra with grace and compassion. Quite simply, happiness is a spiritual experience.

Today, don't let people pull you into their storm. Instead, pull them into your peace and happiness.

August 11

The Universe if helping you and giving you messages every day of your life.

You're exactly who you're supposed to be, where you're supposed to be and doing what you're supposed to be doing. Every day is a spiritual experience for you to learn and grow from. Every day you are receiving messages to help you with these spiritual experiences and you should learn and grow from these.

Sometimes, the quieter you become, the more you can hear. Today, listen, not to just the words people are saying, but also to the messages the Universe is giving you.

August 12

Freedom of choice is free will.

You all have free will and can choose to do almost anything you wish. There is no situation in life where you do not have a choice. Sometimes it takes a great amount of courage and strength to make the right decisions in life. You have the courage of conviction and power of spirit to make any decision necessary to lead you on a good karmic path when you are mindful of your spiritual lessons. There is a positive karmic piggy bank and a negative karmic piggy bank. At the end of your life it is important that your thoughts, words, and actions have a positive and conscious influence on all that you do.

What one thing can you chose to do today that will change your life and make it better?

August 13

Begin each day with this thought:

"Today my every word, thought, and action will be as my Angels, Guides, or higher power would want for my highest good." This simple reminder will keep you conscious of your spiritual principles that you should be incorporating into your life, such as the Law of One and the Golden Rule.

Today, be yourself for you are putting something wonderful in the world today that was not there before.

August 14

Thoughts are just as important as actions.

Every thought that you have, every word that you speak either adds to or takes away from the light of humanity. Everything that you think and say about yourself, whether it is silently to yourself or aloud to others, either adds to or takes away from the light of humanity. Everything that you think and say to and about others, whether it is silently to yourself or aloud to others, either adds to or takes away from the light of humanity. There are no insignificant thoughts or words; each one has energy and an effect.

Today, think compassionate thoughts to all, even those who are not compassionate to you.

August 15

Live by the Law of One.

If you hurt someone else or the environment, you are only hurting yourself. You should always live by the Law of One with loving tolerance for all people in all walks of life on this Earth. Don't wait for the last tree to die, the last river to be poisoned, and the last fish to be caught to realize that you can change this world and your life. You are all connected to each other on this Earth and you should strive to live for the highest good of all.

Today, meditate and connect your heart chakras to the earth and feel a sense of peace and well-being.

August 16

All karmic debts must be paid in full.

A karmic debt is a debt that you have accumulated either in this life or in a past life. It is typically the result of something that occurred between someone else and yourself or from an interaction between the planet and yourself. All karmic debts must be paid either in your present life or in a future life. An example of a karmic debt may be someone who dedicated a career to cutting down trees or something else that harmed the environment in one of his/her past lives. This individual would then have to balance and pay this karmic debt by having a career or volunteering in a field or profession that involved healing or helping the environment or planet in some way.

Learn your karmic lessons today so you can raise your vibrational frequency, consciousness, and move on to your next spiritual lesson.

August 17

The wounded healer heals.

Sometimes, the more pain and suffering you have in your life, the more you can connect to humanity and the concept of oneness, the more you have a chance to heal and to help others heal through your own pain and suffering. It takes immeasurable strength and courage to heal yourself then help others, but strength and courage lives within each of you.

No spiritual lesson ever goes away until it has taught you what you need to know.

August 18

Let your dreams inspire you and your thoughts in meditation guide you.

Your Angels and Guides can visit you in dreams, inspire you with thoughts or, in some cases, speak to you directly during meditation. Whether it is your Angels or Guides, your team will help guide you through your life. They are always there, you just need ask for help and guidance.

Today, never be afraid of failure because your experiences are just temporary spiritual lessons on the path to your dreams and inspiring you to make them come true.

A DAY IN SPIRIT

August 19

Count your joys and blessings.

Don't take your joys and blessings for granted and start grumbling about what you do not have without seeing the true joy of the true blessings that surround you at all times. There are many unfortunate people in this world and it is important to count every blessing that you have. Gratitude unlocks the fullness of life. It turns what you have into enough, and more. It turns denial into acceptance, chaos to order, and confusion to clarity. It can also turn a meal into a feast, a house into a home, a stranger into a friend.

Write down the blessings you have in your life and how those blessings bring you joy.

August 20

Make decisions that move you closer to your spirituality.

At every moment in your life you make choices that will either lead you closer to or further away from remembering the spiritual essence of who you truly are. When you choose to awaken your true self, you ascend further into higher dimensional consciousness as you progress on the path of your spiritual evolution.

Today, know that the center of the Universe is deep within you and dwells in your spirit. You have the ability to change your destiny by tapping into your spirit.

August 21

Mind your karmic debts.

It is important to always remember that each thought, word, and action that you have either adds a coin into your "positive karma" piggy bank or your "negative karma" piggy bank. You want to make it a goal, that at the end of your life, you have more coins in your positive karma piggy bank. Kind words of understanding and even just lending an ear to someone, are all ways to get those positive coins.

Try and do something that is in service of someone else or the environment today.

August 22

Live your life in awareness.

Awareness is a term referring to your ability to perceive, to feel or to be conscious of events, objects, or patterns. Awareness does not necessarily imply understanding nor does being aware mean that you are conscious. If you see a Coke can in a grocery store parking lot, you are aware that it is there. If you pick it up, bring it home, and put it in a recycling bin, then you are conscious of it.

Today, understand that you are here on a newer energy grid and must live your life in higher consciousness and awareness. Write down how you were in a state of awareness today.

August 23

Look for the commonalities.

As you become more spiritually aware, you realize that you live by the Law of One. This law reminds you to look for the commonalities you have with each other and not the differences. It encourages you to build bridges that show you that you are connected to other people and all living and non–living things in life.

Today, recognize that you come from Spirit and must share this planet, our Earth, in peace and harmony and in loving tolerance of others' differences.

August 24

The journey of your life makes you who you are.

It is said that it is not the destination in life but the journey that makes you who you are. The trip itself is not about knowing but about experiencing. These experiences are your only purpose; they are what life is. It is in living each physical life and the experiences it has to offer that is crucial for you to advance in your spiritual lessons and your spiritual evolution.

Today, understand that you can only be what you give yourself the permission and the power to be. Give yourself the permission and the power to soar towards happiness and success in your life.

August 25

Experience the joy of living.

Know that the joy of your life, the joy of living, is nothing more than a buffet of experiences that you can choose from. These experiences, positive or negative, give you the opportunity to expand not just your awareness but also your knowledge and wisdom.

Forget your past, don't think of tomorrow, live in the present moment and find the joy and happiness in this moment today.

August 26

Embrace who you really are.

Part of life is about embracing who you really are and dispelling the thought that you are separate from your spirit. Embracing who you really are also is about bringing the higher and lower aspects of your being into complete harmony and alignment with your higher self or higher purpose in life. You have a great spirit within you and a great light that shines throughout your whole being.

Hold your head up high today and be proud of who you are. Be tall as the trees, strong as the mountains, gentle as the breeze, and warm as the summer rain.

August 27

Pray, meditate, and practice good karma.

Prayer, meditation, reading, and practicing good karma are all ways to help raise your vibrational frequency and awareness. By calming your minds, expanding your knowledge, and working on your spiritual lessons, you can bring yourself closer to the spiritual mastery you are seeking to obtain with each life that you live.

Today, pray, meditate, and practice good karma.

A DAY IN SPIRIT

AUGUST

August 28

What is your life's purpose?

People often ask, "What is my life's purpose?" Your life's purpose can be learned by communication with your Angels and Guides. By raising vibrational frequencies to a higher level, it becomes easier to communicate with your higher self, your Angels, and your Guides who are here loving you and helping you to discover your life's purpose. Your Angels and Guides work hard on helping you discover who you are, why you are here, and what gifts and talents you have to offer humanity and this Earth.

Open your mind today and explore new possibilities for your spiritual progression and purpose. Write down what you think your life's purpose may be.

August 29

Appreciate and enjoy what you already have.

Enjoy whatever amount of success you have achieved instead of feeling sad about what you have not been able to achieve. Living in the present moment and appreciating whatever you have accomplished in that moment is a sign of spiritual advancement. A great philosopher Lao Tzu once said, "If you realize that you have enough, you are truly rich."

What do you appreciate in this moment, right now in your life?

August 30

A higher power exists and you are connected to a Divine source.

Most of you feel that a higher power exists and that you are all connected to a Divine source of some kind. Many of you in the world today are focusing on spiritual development and attaining enlightenment in growing numbers. You will soon come to realize, through your consciousness, that you all worship similar things in different forms and approaches, and you are all of the same essence. There will be a time when you recognize a great conscious awakening among you, one where life will be lived without war and hatred but, instead, lived with love and compassion.

Today, your journey is about unbecoming everything that really isn't you so you can be and become who you are meant to be by a connection through your Divine source.

August 31, 2016

In order to be in a place of higher dimensional consciousness, you must become fully conscious.

Doing this means stopping old patterns and habits that prevent you from living in heightened awareness. Archaic systems no longer serve the good of humanity, and you must stop and change these systems or you will fail on a global level. These changes will bring you into the light of higher conscious awareness. There are many means for bringing limited aspects of yourself into the light of higher consciousness, and your Angels are tirelessly working on this to help you.

Today, expand your consciousness. You are not a drop in the ocean; you are the entire ocean in a drop.

AUGUST

A DAY IN SPIRIT

SEPTEMBER

September 1

Keep the feeling of oneness.

Oneness is often experienced as a feeling that everything is part of a whole or that you all come from one common source, share a common spirit, and are all connected. If you hurt someone, something, or the environment—you are only hurting yourself. This is the feeling of "oneness."

Today, ask for knowledge from your Angels and Guides so you can spread kindness to others.

September 2

Challenging things that happen to you in life serve a very important purpose.

This important purpose is to help you and the world around you with your spiritual evolution. If you look at challenging situations in your life, you can understand that at the end of your life's work, both your positive and negative experiences are all for your highest good. Conversely, through the experience of spiritual consciousness, you begin to see that many things you perceive as good may not be truly good and may just be expressions of your desires, attachments, preferences, or karmic balancing.

What will you learn through your experiences today? Some experiences may be difficult and with obstacles, other experiences may be encouraging and cleansing. Grow, learn, and become wiser from both of these paths.

September 3

You are in a doorway of new opportunities.

You will experience doorways to a new beginnings or opportunities in your life. If you can carry into your daily life a consciousness that goes beyond positive and negative, you will be able to operate from a more centered platform. This will enable you to make better decisions for yourself and grow from your experiences as you see your world with greater clarity and deeper insights.

You will not be the same person you are today as you were yesterday. You are an ever-evolving soul each day of your life through your new opportunities.

September 4

Karma teaches you to live in peace.

Positive and negative karma refers to actual positive or negative actions. It also refers to an intent or motive. For example, even if you do the smallest daily action or deed with great love in your heart, you can change your life from one of constantly creating negative karma to one of constantly creating good karma. Mother Teresa said, "If you have no peace, it is because you have forgotten that you belong to each other." It is important to live your life in peace, harmony, and good karma in order to learn your spiritual lessons and complete your spiritual evolution.

Spiritual experiences will unfold more quickly when you are flexible, spontaneous, and detached. Be those things today. ,

September 5

Develop your spirit.

Your own consciousness is a reflection of the development of your spirit. Understanding the reason for your human existence gives rise to understanding why you go through various positive or negative experiences, why lessons continue to repeat themselves within your life, and why you must learn to overcome your fears and resistances versus remaining a victim to yourself and these fears.

Find your experiences today that can open your eyes and hearts to specific aspects of your life that will allow wisdom and love to lead you in your spiritual growth.

September 6

Your spiritual evolution is why you are here.

The relationship to your own consciousness is a direct relationship to the development of your spiritual evolution. Your spiritual evolution is why you are here and why you have been coming back here over and over again. Living your life in consciousness will always bring you closer to this process and your spiritual mastery.

Today, find new and positive ways to think and see the world in all its potential. Then, you can master a new way of being that will help you with your spiritual growth and evolution.

September 7

Recognize that your ego is not beneficial for you.

It is important to recognize that your ego is not beneficial for you—that it causes much unneeded and unwanted suffering. Your spiritual truth asks the question, "How much suffering will it take for you to recognize who you are, why you are here, and to join hands as brothers and sisters of humanity?" Ego operates out of fear and robs you of your peace and wholeness. Decisions in your life should be made from the heart and from a state of compassion. This will allow you to raise your vibrational frequency and grow and learn in your spiritual lessons and spiritual evolution.

You're world is how you see it. Not necessarily how it actually is. See your truth today, not through your ego, but from a place in your heart.

September 8

Fate is in your hands.

You can begin at this moment to live a happier, more fulfilled life, one that adds a vast amount of happiness to your spirit. Make the decision to change your fate today and visualize a life filled with incredible people and self–mastery as fate is in your hands and can so easily be changed for the better.

When fate gives you difficult times and you wonder where your Angels and Guides are, remember that the teacher is always quiet during a test or in this case, your spiritual lesson.

September 9

Cultivate knowledge, wisdom, and compassion in your life.

As you learn your spiritual lessons you will cultivate knowledge, wisdom, and compassion. Through this you will truly know and understand all that exists and see that we are all one and not two, three, four, etc. Experiences will have clearer meaning and better understanding to you. Having greater insight also allows you to see all you experience from a higher or more elevated platform, which will enable you to spiritually advance more quickly.

Today, cultivate these areas of your life.

A DAY IN SPIRIT

September 10

What is your role in the Universe?

Your role is to reflect harmony, peace, and oneness into the Universe. This, in turn, will help all of humanity raise their vibrational frequencies and help spread peace around the world.

Today, look at a blade of grass, a leaf, a raindrop or whatever seems trivial to you, and see the Universe that lies within it.

September 11

What is your vibrational frequency?

A vibrational frequency is the rate at which atoms and sub-particles of a being vibrate. The higher this vibrational frequency is, the closer it is to the frequency of light. Your words and thoughts send out a vibration that attracts an experience of a similar vibration. If you send out fear, you attract fear. If you send out love, you attract love. Your are a soul with a higher purpose and higher vibrational frequency.

Today, try to raise your vibrational frequency.

September 12

Don't forget to meditate today.

Guided meditations are a wonderful way to calm the mind. It is wonderful to allow your own inner silence and truth, which will help you to relax, unwind, and to live a life full of possibilities that you have created for yourself.

Today, let compassion blossom through meditation. Manifest your compassion and let it shine within your soul.

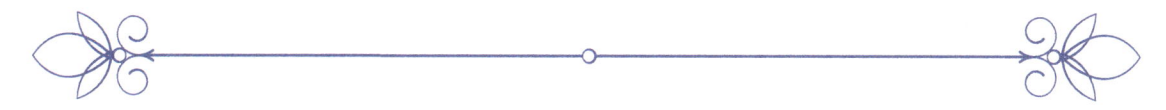

September 13

Clear your negative energy and old emotions.

Clear out any negative energy and old emotions and free yourself up to take on your new day. Try this blessing, "Dear higher power, please bless me and change me with energy to bring healing and balance to my complete being, physically, emotionally, mentally, and spiritually." This simple blessing will help clear negative energy and emotions from your spirit.

Today, understand that the instant you feel anger in controversy, you have ceased striving for the truth and beauty in that situation. Clear out these negative and old emotions.

September 14

Be the light of humanity.

Yes, your thoughts and words do make a difference on this Earth, and each one is important. Each person is as important as another in spreading the light to others. Even your smallest judgmental thought has an effect on your world and all living things on it. You have a great light that beams within you.

Today, be the light and share that light with all that cross your path.

September 15

Did you know karma means action?

Karma is a Sanskrit word from the root "Kri," which means to make or to do. Karma simply means action. It operates in the Universe as the continuous chain reaction of cause and effect. Karma means that "as you sow, so shall you reap" in this and any other lifetime until you understand the complete consequences of all your actions.

Make a choice today that all decisions and actions you make will lead you closer to Spirit.

September 16

You are the change you want to see.

The planet has reached a crisis of epoch proportions and you are the change that is so desperately needed. You are shifting your consciousness and making us all aware of what you are doing to yourself and how you need to change your life to create more nourishing, peaceful, and loving situations. Your Angels and Guides hear your prayers of change today. When you are weak you are given strength and when you are suffering you are comforted by their endless love for you.

You wish to see change today? Be that change. Write down your thoughts on what you think needs change.

September 17

Don't forget to play and laugh.

As children, you play exuberantly. You have fun, enjoy yourself, and have lots of energy. Then something happens. You grow up and you no longer play, believing that adults have to act like adults and adults don't play. Playing is one of your greatest joys and sources of pleasure in life. It takes many forms, from sports to games to laughing and joking with friends. Playing increases your energy and keeps you in a positive frame of mind. It makes those around you more positive and generally lifts the spirits of all involved.

Remember, there are times to be serious, yes, but there are times to play, too, and that is what you must remember. What are you playing and laughing about today?

September 18

You are empowered with special gifts.

One of these special gifts is the Universal Law of Creation, which states, "What you dwell upon, you create." The most pressing issues demand your attention first. If these issues continue to repeat themselves, then you put your energy into eliminating them one at a time. These scenarios might include people, situations, or complex problems that "just won't go away." Instead of fighting them, decide what you can do to solve these issues. See yourself doing just that and then wrapping the healed situation in love and light.

Use your special gift of manifestation today. Remember, what you dwell upon, you create, so dwell upon and create positive circumstances and positive interactions.

A DAY IN SPIRIT

September 19

Live the life you have chosen.

You can have a powerful effect on humanity just by living the life that you have chosen in spirit with love and compassion in your heart. Yes, you will go through hard times, filled with spiritual lessons and experiences, but you will also have great joy and happiness. This is what healing and evolving through spirit is about—finding and acknowledging the great gifts you have within your souls and sharing them with others.

Find and acknowledge the great gifts you hold within your soul and let those gifts soar into the Universe.

September 20

Practice Aagami karma.

Aagami karma is your future karma. It is the karmic map that is coming as a result of the merits and demerits of the present thoughts, actions, and words of your current birth. It is the portion of actions in the present life that can add to or subtract from your Sanchita karma or cosmic karma. If you fail to work off your debt, then more debts are added to Aagami karma and are brought forward to work off in future lives.

When you are inspired to be and do your best, you find everything will be right in your world. Be and do your best today to help your Aagami karma.

September 21

Stop living in the past; live in the present moment.

In disagreements with others, deal only with the current situation. Don't bring up the past as the past is over and gone. Yesterday provided you with many valuable lessons. Learn from them, or they will be repeated until you do. Live in the now, this present moment. Yesterday and tomorrow can be turned over to the Universe, but the present moment is yours to live in with great clarity and happiness. Living in the present moment creates happiness.

Today, try simple exercises such as deep breathing and visualization techniques. This will allow you to live in the present moment, a moment of happiness.

September 22

Every day, work on your spiritual experiences.

As souls, you experience constant cycles of births and deaths into a series of bodies until you have learned all the spiritual lessons that the totality of all your experiences have to teach you. Every day you are working on these experiences via physical and spiritual forces in the Universe. Physical, spiritual, and mental thoughts and actions are never lost but are transformed and played out through your soul's spirit.

Today, remember, stars cannot shine without darkness and you cannot shine in the light without going through the dark and this is done through your spiritual experiences.

September 23

You are releasing energy into the Universe and are affected by energy coming in.

Through your thoughts, actions and words, you are releasing spiritual energy to the Universe and are, in turn, affected by influences or energies coming in to you from all directions. You are your own sender and receiver of your thoughts, actions, and energy. As you sow, so shall you reap in this or any other lifetime. Any of your physical actions or thoughts can change your energy. Negative actions and thoughts create negative energy; positive actions and thoughts create positive energy. Sometimes you are taken into troubled waters not to struggle, but to cleanse your spirit.

What troubled waters need to be cleansed in your life today to help your energy?

September 24

You are a radiant soul.

You are able to fulfill your purpose just by being the radiant soul that you are. There is no way that you cannot be who you are as a soul, and so your purpose is unfolding with every breath that you take. You are a part of the living web of life here on Earth, and each soul within that web is a part of the whole, unique, and divine plan for all of humanity.

Remember, it does not require many words to know and speak your truth of who you are and why you're here on Earth spreading your soul's radiant wisdom to all.

September 25

You will attract people who have the same or similar karma that you have.

If you physically fight others, you may attract this type of individual over and over. Until you become aware and conscious of your own behavior and want to change it, you will stay in the same karmic pattern. Until you start to strive for change and a more peaceful environment, you will be stuck in negative karmic cycles, repeating them until your spiritual lessons are learned.

Today, be a beacon of light by responding to hate with loving compassion and accepting all who walk this Earth with love.

September 26

All your energy is constantly rippling through the Universe.

Your thoughts and emotions, no matter how private you may consider them, affect others around you. You are a result of the energy you create from your thoughts and actions, which, again, contributes to your karmic balance sheet. This energy is also part of your aura and affects everything around you, including your family, friends, the world, and even the Universe.

Today, respond to hatred with love. Let go of all thoughts of aggression and revenge, and beckon the higher side of you to reach out with love in your heart, kindness in your soul, and peace within your being.

September 27

The law of karma affects all that is.

It also affects all that you do toward anyone or anything—including humans, animals, plants, planets, and beings of any nature. Every action, thought, and emotion is energy, and this radiates into the Universe like a radio station. Some people may radiate thoughts and feelings of love that raise their vibrational frequency. Some may cause mental or emotional stress to others that may cause mental or emotional pain, which lowers their vibrational frequency.

Today, look to your past and see gratitude, look forward and see your vision, look upwards and fill your spirit, and look within to find your peace.

A DAY IN SPIRIT

September 28

Be aware of all your thoughts and emotions.

Living in awareness will help you to create positive energy in your life. You must be prepared to receive the kind of energy you radiate both physically and in your thoughts and minds. Thoughts of love and good will towards others will bring you the same in return.

Today, try to stay positive with your thoughts and emotions.

September 29

Meditating is important.

If you throw a stone into a stormy ocean with rough waves, you probably won't be able to see any ripples made by that stone. Think of the stone as a thought and the stormy ocean as your mind filled with clutter. If the stone/thought is tossed into a stormy ocean/cluttered mind, the effects of the stone landing in the rough water could not be seen. However, if you were to calm that stormy ocean or your mind like a peaceful, calm pond and you threw the stone or thought into it, the ripples would be seen to the very edge of the pond. By calming your minds and thinking peaceful or happy thoughts, the effects or ripples from these tranquil and contented thoughts can be felt by all.

Let conscious breathing be your anchor today. Thoughts and feelings come and go and your soul must be anchored in consciousness through meditation.

September 30

Karma teaches you conscious awareness.

Every thought that you have and every word that you speak either adds to or takes away from the light of humanity. Everything that you think and say about yourself, whether it is silently to yourself or aloud to others, either adds to or takes away from the light of humanity. Everything that you think and say to and about others, whether it is silently to yourself or aloud to others, either adds to or takes away from the light of humanity. There are no insignificant thoughts or words; each one has energy and an effect. Living your life in conscious awareness helps you to live in the light and be one with the Universe.

Today, understand that being spiritual has nothing to do with what you believe in and everything to do with your state of conscious awareness.

A DAY IN SPIRIT

OCTOBER

October 1

As you spiritually progress, so will your willingness to serve humanity.

Perfection is a state of total selflessness. As you spiritually progress in your life, all desire for physical pleasures is replaced by a complete dedication to serve humanity or help this Earth in some way. This is a sign of a spiritually progressing soul.

Today, touch someone with your spirit by helping them in some way, and in turn, they will touch you with their heart.

October 2

Know the Law of Karma.

The law of karma is very simple. It states, "Whatever you do to others will be done to you in this or any future incarnation of your soul." Is it not amazing that one of the most beautiful compensations in life is knowing that not one soul can try to help another without helping himself/herself?

Ask yourself, what is your spiritual lesson today?

October 3

There is positive and/or negative in every thought, action, and word you produce.

You are given the opportunity to shape yourself into beautiful, peaceful, fulfilled, loving, and selfless individuals. In order to do this, you need to make your thoughts, actions, and words come from a place of love.

Today when you wake up, realize that someone else is breathing their last breath. Make today count, make today beautiful, and make today a glorious wonder.

October 4
Let fear go from your life.

Fear is a horrible and highly contagious disease that can hold you back in your life and allow others to control you. This extends to family, friends, co-workers, the government, and even terrorists. Don't let anyone control you through fear as you have great power within your spirit to lead your own life in peace, harmony, and your own truth.

Do you wish to know a secret? To exist is to have no fear. Fear nothing today and let no one instill fear in you.

October 5
Never judge others; it lowers your vibrational frequency.

Never judge others; you don't know what their life's purpose is or what their Angels and Guides have planned for them. Being judgmental also lowers your vibrational frequency and keeps you away from your higher power, your Guides, and your Angels. Take a new road today to seek your spiritual fulfillment and happiness that has nothing to do with judging others. Not everyone will be on the same road as you as we are all on different roads in our spiritual evolution.

Today, don't judge others who are in different stages of their soul's evolution. Live the day with love, compassion, and loving tolerance of what is different from you.

October 6
Karma teaches you to live your life with love.

You should live your life in love of others and for others without any expectation of repayment. You should live your life in love, forgiving hurts against you, asking for the consolation of dead relatives and friends, and loving everyone with no distinction between friend and foe. This brings about true lasting joy and happiness, good karma and virtue to yourself, your loved ones, and the world. If you are kind to others, even those who are not kind to you, you will find true happiness. This begins by living your life with love.

Today, love and be loved. Write down people you love, what you love about them, and how you love yourself.

October 7

It's all about universal balance.

It is important to keep your life in balance. Remember what goes around comes around; you reap what you sow. Keep your life in balance by maintaining good thoughts towards humanity and this Earth and keep yourself in balance.

Today, know that not only do your Angels and Guides love you as much as anybody in the entire Universe, but you, yourself, as much as anybody in the Universe, deserves your own love. These blessings will help keep you in balance.

October 8

Serve others and serve the earth.

Your Angels are most proud of you when you are in service to others and the earth. The process is something like this: as you serve, you draw energy to yourself. By giving energy, you get energy and as you serve, you demonstrate love. Love is the way and all there is. Being in service to others or the environment is also the fastest way to raise your vibrational frequency and clear karmic debt.

Today, treat the earth well and know that it was not given to you by your parents, it was loaned to you by Mother Earth and you are merely one of its caretakers.

October 9

Develop through your spiritual evolution.

The development of your own awareness, consciousness, and ascension has a direct relationship to the development of your spiritual evolution. You can arise and awaken within your consciousness your memories of all lives you have lived. You can arise and awaken to your true meaning and your true spiritual purpose. You can arise and awaken to the joys and wonders of this life and your spiritual evolution.

Today, treat those who are good today with goodness and treat those who are not good with love, kindness, and understanding.

A DAY IN SPIRIT

October 10

Heal and evolve through spirit.

Healing and evolving through spirit awakens your souls and uplifts your consciousness so you can make huge advancements in your spiritual evolution. Work on healing the pain that lies within you. Feel love in your heart and know that you are never alone as your Angels and Guides are always with you giving you messages of love to inspire your spiritual growth and advancement.

Today, make your spiritual journey about unlearning fear and accepting love and healing and evolving through your spirit.

October 11

Karma lives in the law of cause and effect.

The law of cause and effect basically states that for every movement of energy that takes the form of an image, feeling, desire, belief, expectation or action, there is a corresponding effect. For this reason, the law of cause and effect influences every aspect of your karma. In order to make the most of the law of cause and effect, you must live consciously and recognize that you are the creator of your own reality.

Today, make a karmic goal to ensure that you link your actions (the cause) with their results (the effect). Write down one example of this that occurred in your day today.

October 12

Practice saying, "I'm sorry" and "I forgive you."

Without pain, most of you wouldn't learn about dimensional consciousness and how to grow peace from a quiet place within your souls. Saying "I'm sorry" or "I forgive you" is not easy. There are always spiritual lessons in your life, and, in most cases, you will be unable to move on or remove obstacles from your paths until these lessons are learned. Forgiving will free up your spiritual energy and help you with these spiritual lessons and learning to forgive is the first step.

All that you are today is a result of what you have forgiven. Make your thoughts powerful and positive by walking, living, and breathing in the glorious light of who you are.

October 13
Practice forgiveness.

Being able to forgive is hard to do. It takes incredible strength, a courageous spirit, and great inner love; but the simple act of forgiveness can create great healing within your soul.

Today, realize life isn't the way you want it to be, it is the way your Angels and Guides want you to learn and grow from your lessons and this starts with forgiveness.

October 14
Follow your road map.

Your Angels will arrange to help you as much as they can to help you find out what your purpose is in life. Pull back from your situations and look at the bigger picture. Asking, "Why am I here, what is my life's purpose, and how can I contribute to humanity?" is a good place to start when finding out what your road map is.

Today, ask for the strength of Angel's wings, for faith and courage to fly to new heights, and the wisdom of the Universe to carry you there on your road map to who you are supposed to be and what you are supposed to do in this life.

October 15
You have a powerful effect on humanity.

You can have a powerful effect on humanity just by living the life that you have chosen and by going through hard times, spiritual lessons, and experiences with love and compassion in your heart. Each one of you is important in the web of life and each one of you has great contributions to make that will have a great impact and will make a difference to others and this Earth.

Let light in your heart today so you can find your way to discovering your spirit in all its beauty and glory and the effect you have on humanity.

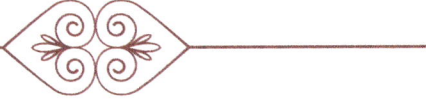

October 16

Heal and evolve through your spirit.

Healing and evolving through spirit is about finding and acknowledging the great gifts you have within your soul. You have an endless storage of gifts within yourself that are waiting to emerge with your spiritual advancement.

Allow yourself to be loved today for it will give you strength. Allow yourself to love someone else as well for it will give you the courage to heal and evolve through your spirit.

October 17

Find your gift.

By finding the gifts that have come to you as a result of your consciousness and awareness and sharing these gifts and realizations with others, your own life's purpose about why you are here, and what you have to contribute can unfold. You have an endless amount of wonderful gifts within yourself. Enjoy discovering them.

Today find the inner peace and wisdom that is needed to discover the gifts you have within yourself.

October 18

Savor the joys of your achievements.

It is one thing to achieve your goal; it is another to enjoy it after you have achieved it. There are two things to aim at in life: first, to achieve the goals the goals you have set; and after that, to enjoy it. Only the wisest of souls can achieve the second and you are this wise soul.

Enjoy all goals in your life, both big and small.

A DAY IN SPIRIT

October 19

Your Angels and Guides are always with you.

Your Angels and Guides are always with you during your journey in life. They are always within your touch, sight, and hearing as they offer gentle reminders of who you are, why you're here, and how to find your way in this crazy life on Earth.

Ask your Angels and Guides to reveal the lessons you are here to learn that may be hidden under every leaf and rock you may see.

October 20

Your Guardian Angels are not separate from you.

Your Guardian Angels are not separate from you. They are dedicated to you and travel with you everywhere you go and are with you at all times. They have made an agreement with your soul to assist you in completing any of the tasks or lessons you have decided to undertake in each and every life.

Today, recognize that you are not alone and feel the love and protection that is being given to you.

October 21

What you dwell on, you manifest.

Whatever you think, speak, or act on becomes your reality. Thoughts become words. Words become actions. Actions become values. Make sure to think, speak, and act in a positive way.

Manifesting peace, happiness, and tranquility with your Angels and Guides will be your most important conversation today. Are you dwelling on positive thoughts?

October 22

Let group consciousness and group awareness be your path.

You are all equal here on this Earth. No one person is greater than any other. Group consciousness and awareness is the path to the future. You must learn to function cooperatively for the good of all to change the energy and create a civilization that is more desirable. Changes in the outdated systems that no longer serve the good of humanity begin with groups of people wanting to change these systems.

Today, join or post a message on a group, any group, even on Facebook or Twitter that wants to make a difference.

October 23

Karma is the Universal law of cause and effect.

Karma is the universal law of cause and effect, action and reaction, total cosmic justice, and personal responsibility. "A good cause, a good effect; a bad cause, a bad effect" is a common saying when referring to karma. Karma works on both action and thought, and this is why it is important for you to train your mind to think positive thoughts no matter what situations you encounter along your life's journeys.

A sign of your spiritual strength and evolution is how you respond to weakness, inexperience, and the offensive actions of others. Are you positive, forgiving, and loving?

October 24

You contain many messages within your hearts.

The messages that you hold are contained within your hearts. As a group you are working to help humanity to open its collective heart chakra and embrace higher energy and higher consciousness. Share and spread your messages.

Today, feel all the beautiful things contained within your soul. Write some of these down.

October 25

Seek happiness and contentment in the present moment.

Do not associate happiness with future events. It is like postponing your happiness to an unsure future. The time to be happy is today, because yesterday has already passed and the only thing that matters is the happy moment that is happening now. How simple it is to see that you can be happy now, and there will never be a time when it is not now.

Live in your current moment and be happy in that moment.

October 26

Hold your light on yourself and others.

It is important to hold the light not only on yourself, but also on those who will not, can't, or don't know how to hold the light upon themselves. You made an agreement before you were born as to what your purpose is and how you were going to live out your life to achieve that purpose and help humanity. Others may not understand this message and it's important for you to hold the light for both yourself and for them.

Today, hold your light and laugh your heart out, dance in the rain, cherish each moment, ignore the pain, live in the moment, laugh at every possible moment, and love all that you encounter.

October 27

Be kind to all, even those who are not kind to you.

It is hard to know or understand each soul's life purpose or what role they play in the Divine Plan of things. So be careful not to judge others and be kind to all, even people who are not kind to you.

Give love and kindness to all today.

A DAY IN SPIRIT

October 28

Draw strength and courage from just being who you are.

Every second of every day, know that you are a beautiful and worthy being. Know that you are blessing to humanity and are here for a purpose. You are important and you are here for a reason.

Today, overcome fear that may be holding you back in life. Draw strength and courage from within your own spirit.

October 29

Your path may be difficult, but you are strong.

Your path may be a hard one but you have chosen this because you are a soul who has the strength and the wisdom for this task. This Earth and the people on it are lucky to have you here helping. Never give up on your purpose and keep hope and faith always on your side.

Try not to worry, be impatient, or criticize anything today for worry is falling short of faith, impatience is falling short of kindness, and criticism falls short of love. Your spirit is strong enough to overcome this.

October 30

Remember that there is a "positive karma" piggy bank and a "negative karma" piggy bank.

Every good action and thought puts a coin in either your positive karma piggy bank or your negative karma piggy bank. Reflect on how many positive and negative thoughts you have during the day. Make both your thoughts and actions as positive as you can. This pattern will be reflected in your energy. Positive thoughts and actions will bring you good karma in this life.

Spirit will always give back more then what you have given to it. Enjoy your good karma by harvesting the miracles that surround you today.

October 31

May the force be with you.

There should be a tag that you have to tear off every child after they are born before you can hold them. This tag should read: Caution: This is not a vulnerable soul that needs to be controlled and shaped. Please learn from the wisdom and gifts this child brings you. Cannot be returned or exchanged. May the force be with you. Do not be afraid of tomorrow and let go of yesterday. Tomorrow does not exist and yesterday is gone. The only thing that matters are what you are thinking, feeling, and doing today.

Today, be a positive force to be reckoned with. Your force is with you.

OCTOBER

A DAY IN SPIRIT

NOVEMBER

November 1

Your body is your temple, honor it.

Keep the temple of your body neat, clean, and healthy. Do not dump garbage of dirty, negative thoughts, and toxic junk in it. There is a close relationship between the mind, body, and spirit. By taking care of your body, you will also be taking care of your mind and spirit.

Today, be mindful of the food you eat and how much exercise you are participating in.

November 2

You are a spiritual warrior.

You are a spiritual warrior who is assisting this Earth by clearing old systems and outdated beliefs so that new systems and beliefs can be created. You are the systems–busters who will liberate all from their old ways of thinking.

Be in the light today. When a light switch is turned on, darkness has nowhere to go but away from your soul because you are a spiritual warrior here to help humanity.

November 3

You are the light of humanity through your thoughts, words, and actions.

When your thoughts and words come from a place of unconditional love, which means that they are without judgment, they spread light and increase the light and vibrational frequency on the planet.

Today, know you are the light of humanity and you are special.

November 4
Focus on changing yourself and this will help change the world around you.

It is impossible to change the world around you. So stop fretting when people do not come up to your expectations. The best course is to change yourself right now in this moment. Never underestimate the power you have to change yourself as it is surprising how changing yourself can change others around you.

Change one thing today. See something in a more positive light and watch how this changes how you see the world.

November 5
Your love is the energy that gives and maintains life.

Love is the emotion that binds you to each other as well as the energy that gives and maintains life. You must direct your thoughts and words through your heart chakras before speaking or acting. Can you see the hurt and pain in others? Share the power of your heart chakras with them and watch how it can change another's life.

Take time to share your love and energy today. Write down how you are doing this.

November 6
Great spiritual growth comes through faith.

Faith plays a significant role in your spiritual awareness and spiritual growth and sometimes spiritual growth means taking a leap of faith from time to time. Rather than trying to get everything in place before you start something important, why not let your path evolve through the guidance of your Angels?

Ask for faith today. With faith comes knowledge and with knowledge you can find kindness for all.

November 7

Your happiest moment is right now.

Hollywood child star Shirley Temple Black once narrated an incident about her husband Charles and his mother. When Charles was a boy he asked his Mom what was the happiest moment in her life. His mother replied, "This moment, right now." The boy further asked, "But what about all the other happy moments in your life, say, when you were married?" His mother replied, "My happiest moment then was then. My happiest moment now is now. You can live your life only in the moment you are in and this requires unflinching faith."

Today, be present and happy in your current moment. Do not live in the past or the future. The present moment is all that exists and you should try to live your life in the moment you are in.

November 8

Be a light and spread your light.

You are a beaming light in the darkness of humanity. Shine your light on all that cross your path. You can also be the light for those who can't, won't, or don't know how to shine the light upon themselves.

If today were your last, would you do what you're doing? Or would you love more, give more, forgive more, and spread your light?

November 9

Each person is important.

You are important, your energy is important and you can make a difference each and every day of your life. Spread your light to everyone you can each and every day of your life. Your Angels will be proud and more importantly, you will make a significant difference in this world.

Today, know you are here for a reason, on a group mission to help all living and non-living things on this Earth. You role is important. You matter more then you may possibly know.

A DAY IN SPIRIT

November 10

You are never alone.

You are never alone in this world. You have a team of Angels and Guides that are with you every moment of your life. They are guiding you, helping you, and loving you through your journey. Listen and feel them with you and take comfort knowing they are here with you.

Today, when you think that nobody understands you and you are alone, remember that you are not. Your team of Angels and Guides are always by your side, loving, guiding, and helping you along your path.

November 11

Your lessons can be hard.

A spiritual lesson may be much more difficult for one soul than another. For example, it may take one soul thirty lifetimes to conquer the emotion of forgiveness and another soul just one. It isn't a race, but if you become more conscious, you can live your life with more awareness of its true meaning. You cannot spiritually advance without some tough lessons. Learn these lessons and move onto easier ones and understand that the love of the Universe is always with you, helping you, and guiding you.

Today, learn your difficult lessons so you can progress to easier ones. Write down one of these lessons.

November 12

Great karmic strides can be made with intention.

Intention is the most important of all mental processes because it guides the mind in determining how to engage with virtuous, non-virtuous, or neutral objects. Just as iron is powerlessly drawn to a magnet, your minds are drawn to the object of your intentions. An intention is a mental thought or action that may be expressed through either a physical or a verbal action. With intention, what you dwell on, you create and great karmic strides are made through intention.

One of the greatest gifts you can give yourself today is the freedom to learn your own spiritual lessons through intention.

November 13

Your path can and will change.

Your path in life or your life's purpose can and will change at any time. You have free will and this can create a path that can turn in many different directions. It doesn't matter what direction you take, your Angels and Guides will always be there to help and assist you as your lessons will be the same no matter what path you take.

If you don't like something in your life today, change it. If you can't change it, then change the way you think about it.

November 14

The Universe works on the principle of energy.

Your family and friends, who may be in the same soul group, may have similar vibrational frequencies as you do. Looking at lessons being learned by family and friends may help you reach within and look at your own life's lessons and this is based on the principle of energy—like attracts like.

There is a plan for everything in your life and today. Don't spend time worrying, spend time looking at your energy and the energy of those around you.

November 15

Ultimately, you are all connected to each other.

You are all connected with others, your goals, purposes, experiences, energy, and vibrational frequencies are all shared. We all share a common goal, to spiritually advance and a common planet, Earth.

Today, have compassion and inspire others and allow others to have compassion and inspire you.

November 16

Humanity is like a tapestry where all lives are interwoven.

Humanity is like a tapestry where all lives are interwoven like threads weaving together in continuous lines. One thread always affects another to form an intricate picture or lesson. Together, this tapestry creates a picture of how all people are connected to one another in all walks of life no matter of geographic locations.

Today, know the way that you live and the thoughts that you think, will connect you to who you are and who you are to others in this tapestry.

November 17

Live your life in consciousness and gratitude.

By living your life consciously and in gratitude for every living and non-living thing in this world, you will all be able to move forward more quickly with your spiritual lessons. Being conscious allows you to see things as they really are, not as you are. Being grateful for both good and challenging experiences allows you the wisdom to understand that there are lessons in both situations.

Today, be kind, compassionate, and understanding to all that live. This will help you live your life in consciousness and with gratitude.

November 18

Love is always the answer.

Remember, love is always the answer and all that there is. It is what connects us, keeps us compassionate, and helps us with our spiritual lessons. It is that simple.

Today, love yourself as well as others.

A DAY IN SPIRIT

November 19

Raise your vibrational frequency by being grateful.

When you are grateful for both good and challenging things that happen in your life, you are raising your vibrational frequency and rising to a higher spiritual realm and higher dimensional consciousness. Being grateful allows you a kindness and compassion that would otherwise not be found when living your life without gratitude.

Today, know that in your daily life you must see that it is not happiness that makes you grateful, it is gratefulness that makes you happy.

November 20

Be positive and give service to humanity and the earth.

By being positive and giving service to Earth and all things on it, you will be able to change your energy and, therefore, your karma. The fastest way to raise your vibrational frequency and erase bad karma is through service. Being in service to humanity and the earth, allows your soul to be compassionate and understanding of other things and other places around you. This shows spiritual and evolutionary advancement when focusing on others' suffering and the earth's troubles.

Today, stop and truly look around. Because when you stop and look around with a spiritual point of view, you will see how badly the earth and the people on it need your positive energy and influences.

November 21

Change is possible within you.

Change is possible within you and is a part of life. Nothing is stagnant. Is there something that causes you conflict and strife and keeps you from being the positive, contented, happy person that you would like to be? What can you do to change that situation? It doesn't have to be something huge. We all learned to walk by taking one staggering step at a time. You can overcome conflict and hatred, spanning seemingly timeless generations and live in peace. You can grow and rise above limitations in stagnant and outdated non–spiritual beliefs and policies that hurt the world as a whole.

Today, make a decision to change that which causes you conflict and strife and make your life more positive as it is simple to stay positive with a little practice.

November 22

Without exception, you have Angels around you constantly.

Your Angels are eager and excited at the opportunity to communicate with you. You all have one Guardian Angel and at least one to three Angels assigned to you your whole life, but additional Angels will come and go as you work on your spiritual lessons. They never leave your side and are there loving and guiding you throughout your life.

Today, you are loved, not for the sake of being loved that is human. You are loved for the sake of loving and this is your Angels doing this.

November 23

Love is around you every day of your life.

Love is all around you every day of your life; you only need to open your eyes to see it, feel it and experience it. It is patient, kind, and not jealous. Love bears all things, believes all things, hopes all things, and endures all things.

Know you are loved today and that this love is the strongest of all life's passions. Let this love reach into your heart, mind, and soul.

November 24

Create positive energy in your life.

Being aware of all your thoughts and emotions, as well as all your words and actions, will help you to create positive energy in your life. You must be prepared to receive the kind of energy you radiate both physically and in your thoughts and minds.

Try to give off positive energy today so positive energy can boomerang back to you. Write down any of these experiences.

November 25

Practice manifesting one small thing each day.

A good exercise to try is to manifest one small thing that is unusual in your day. You can write down or think about what you want to manifest. Make it something possible but unlikely to happen, such as, "Today I will see a bright green car on the freeway," or "Today I will find a quarter on the street," or "Today I will meet someone from Asia." Be realistic—it just won't be possible to manifest a polar ice cap while living in Mexico. Then wait and see what happens.

Pick one small thing you would like manifest today. Write it down and if it is in your highest good or highest good for others, it will happen.

November 26

Your Guardian Angel was created out of the same essence that makes up your soul.

Your Guardian Angel isn't essentially separate from you. It has absolute and unequivocal dedication and travels with you on every journey that you as a free will entity choose to make. Guardian Angels are also called tutelary Angels because they stay with you, watching over your life, protecting you, and encouraging your spiritual well–being and happiness.

Your Guardian Angel stands by your side each and every day of your life. Today, ask for anything you want or need and wait for its arrival.

November 27

Listen to others.

Take the time to listen to another person—really listen as you look into their eyes—not the "pretend" listening many people do as they look at a person while thinking about what they are going to do with their day. A few minutes of your time will not cost you anything and can mean so much to another soul. This is yet another way to spread your wondrous light onto others.

Take time to really listen and hear someone today. How did that make you feel?

A DAY IN SPIRIT

November 28

There is a poignant and beautiful connection between your heart and your soul.

All your experiences in life can affect both your heart's and soul's spiritual growth. Like all of us, you decided before you came to Earth that you would embody specific energies and situations that humanity is struggling with at this time. As you walk your path in life, you are finding your way by shifting and transmuting your experiences into positive circumstances that help heal all that is.

Find the energies you embody within your heart and soul and make them positive. Write down what some of these energies are.

November 29

Embrace your spiritual lessons.

Be thankful of all lessons in your life as all experiences hold valuable spiritual lessons. Remove the negative aspects and look at the positive. There can be a spiritual lesson every day of your life so live in consciousness and awareness of this. These lessons can be quite small or very big, but they are there each day of your life. You may also be working on many lessons—not just one at a time. Learning how to love is the goal and the purpose of most of these spiritual lessons.

Today, embrace love in all aspects of your life.

November 30

Live life through your heart chakra.

Living through your heart chakra will help you live a more harmonious life even during difficult times. Send all your thoughts, words, and actions through your heart chakra before you think, speak, or take action on any situation. Lashing out in pain to another person will not benefit you or your karma. Shining, understanding, and loving one another will.

Today, be the light and the heart shining in the darkness of the world. Know your love is the bridge between you and everything.

A DAY IN SPIRIT

DECEMBER

December 1

Walk your path.

At every moment in your life you have a choice that will either lead you closer to your spirit or further away from it. Finding your way in life, a road, a path, the way by which people travel is a path to your truth and your ultimate reality of who you are and why you are here. Remember, the future is not someplace you are going, but one you are creating.

Today, do not find your path; be the maker of it and this will change your destination.

December 2

Live your life in spiritual awareness.

Spiritual awareness or spiritual awakening is the process by which you begin to explore your own being in order to become whole and reunite with your true spiritual meaning. By living a life in spiritual awareness, you will better understand your purpose while here on this very difficult Earth.

Today, be spiritually aware of why you are here and what lessons you are meant to learn. Write some of these lessons down.

December 3

Engage in the welfare of humanity.

People of expanded spiritual awareness become engaged in the welfare of humanity. You must realize you have something to give and share with others whether it's money, time, or prayers. Every person makes a difference when contributing to the welfare of others. Collectively, a community, city, state, or country, can change the world for the better.

No one is useless on our Earth who lightens the burdens of others. Lighten someone's burden today.

December 4

Your journey is important.

It is said that it's not the destination in life, but the journey that makes you who you are. The trip itself isn't about knowing, but about experiencing. This is a big part of your spiritual lessons and these experiences are your only purpose—it is what life is. Your Angels and Guides don't want you to forget to have fun and laugh along your journey. So make time for special people in your life, traveling, or whatever brings joy to your heart.

Today, have faith in your journey. Everything is happening exactly as it should to get you where you're going next.

December 5

There is an ultimate goal in spiritual awareness.

The ultimate goal in spiritual awareness is to align with a higher source and keep vibrational frequencies at a higher level to help you live out your life's purpose, and find the special gifts and talents that you have to offer. It is when you break down your true meaning of who you are and why you're here that you truly discover that the milestones in your life are earmarked by happy memories.

Today, keep your awareness on all things surrounding you and let this awareness rest within your own soul.

December 6

Be conscious in your daily life.

To be fully conscious, you must stop old patterns and habits that prevent you from living your life in awareness. Be a good, kind, and honorable person, be kind to all that cross your path, and be grateful for everything that happens in your life.

Define what consciousness means to you.

December 7

Everything is composed of energy.

Physics tells you that everything is composed of energy. Even if you can't see it, energy exists at various frequencies, and is in essence, all things. Your bodies are essential in maintaining the harmony between your physical body and your soul through this energy. Everything is energy.

Today, be aware and conscious of either positive energy or negative energy in your life. Change the energy that does not make you happy.

December 8

Do you feel a higher power exists?

Most people feel that a higher power exists and that you are connected to a Divine power of some kind. People of the world today are focusing on spiritual development, spiritual evolution, and attaining enlightenment. You will soon come to a realization that you all worship the same Source in different forms and approaches, but you are of the same essence. There will be a time when you will recognize a great conscious awakening among you all, where life will be lived without war and hatred and lived in peace and harmony.

Today, tap into you're higher power that guides you and is not separate from you.

December 9

Can you define consciousness?

Consciousness is a difficult term to define, because the word is used and understood in a wide variety of ways. What frequently happens is what one person sees as a definition of consciousness is seen by others as something else altogether. Consciousness may involve thoughts, sensations, perceptions, moods, emotions, dreams, and self–awareness. Sometimes consciousness denotes being awake and responsive to yourself and your environment, in contrast to being unconscious and unaware. In the end, it is always about taking action towards a positive outcome.

Today, write down what you feel consciousness is to you and how it does or does not define you.

A DAY IN SPIRIT

December 10
Do you have a feeling of "oneness?"

Oneness is often experienced as a feeling that everything is part of a whole, or that you all come from one common source, share a common spirit, and are all connected. People, who feel oneness, often live by the Law of One, which states that we are all connected to each other and when you hurt others, you are only hurting yourself through karma.

You are the Universe and any expression of yourself affects all there is. Today, express joy and happiness to all people in all walks of life on this Earth as we are all one.

December 11
You walk with Angels among you.

Angels are dedicated to serving the needs of all spiritual beings so that you may experience the same level of unconditional love as they do. Each Angel carries out its assigned task without any hint of hesitation as they take great joy and pleasure in offering their loving wisdom and guidance to all beings in all Universes. Know that your Angel's loving presence is with you at all times.

Order an Angel today. You don't have to speak words to do this. Just visualize or think "Angels" and they will be there by your side, loving you, guiding you, and keeping you safe.

December 12
An Angel was created to love you and be with you.

Angels were created with one purpose—to love and to serve without conditions. In doing so, Angels hold a focus of pure love throughout the Universe and are able to set up a resonance for the vibration of pure love wherever and whenever it is needed. Your Angels were created to be with you and are always by your side. You are never alone on you path in life.

Say, "Thank you" to your Angels today. They are by your side each day of your life.

December 13

Your Angel will counter balance any energy that is the opposite of love.

Here on Earth, you have free will. This means that you have chosen to gain your experiences through many lifetimes and many varied forms of existence. Your Angels are created to counterbalance any energies or actions that move in the opposite direction to love so that you will remember your true spiritual purpose. Love is all around you every day of your lives; you only need to open your eyes to see it, feel it, and experience it.

Today, ask that beautiful Angels of kindness, abundance and prosperity, shower you with positive energy for continued healing and that your hopes and dreams become reality.

December 14

Your Angel will appear in many shapes and forms.

Angels can appear to you in many forms and shapes. At times, the qualities of an Angel are so delicate that they come in specific forms that will suit your needs. An Angel will often appear to you with the form that is best for you or one that you can understand. So you may see an Angel with wings or one that may look like liquid mercury depending on what you are comfortable with.

Today ask an Angel to show themselves to you, but do not fear an Angel that appears to you in a form that you are not familiar with.

December 15

Karma cultivates knowledge, wisdom, and compassion.

As you learn your spiritual lessons and karmic actions through the processes of reincarnation and karma, you will grow and cultivate your gardens of knowledge, wisdom, and compassion. Though karma may not appear merciful to you, it is the most compassionate and effective way to restore balance and teach your soul your spiritual lessons. You have all made mistakes because you have not always followed the highest voice from within, thus causing suffering to others and ultimately to yourself. The voice of conscience within each of you lets you see the possible results of the right and wrong actions you choose in life. You have knowledge to interpret these actions and the wisdom, compassion, and free will to make choices from this.

What thoughts are you sending out to the Universe today? Are they knowledgeable, wise, and full of compassion?

December 16

You must ask an Angel for help, they cannot do it automatically.

It is important to remember that Angels cannot just come into your life when you need help due to the laws of free will. You must specifically ask for their help. It is also important to be grateful and say thank you for their divine wisdom, love, help, and support in your life because being grateful for both positive and negative things raises your vibrational frequency. When you ask for something, be prepared that it may not come as you expect.

Today, order an Angel for anything and everything you need in your life. Nothing is too trivial. Write down all the Angels you want and need.

December 17

You have a Guardian Angel with you in every life that you have.

A Guardian Angel is an angelic being that is dedicated to serve and to help you throughout your lifetime. This Guardian Angel was created out of the same essence that makes up your soul and is often with you for many lifetimes. They are great spiritual beings with incredible amounts of love and vast amounts of wisdom. You are always loved and never alone.

Today, know you have a Guardian Angel who is loving, kind, and caring and will be there when you need someone to share your burdens in life.

December 18

Angels watch over you each and every day.

Guardian Angels are also called tutelary Angels because they stay with you, watching over your life, protecting you, and encouraging your spiritual well-being and happiness. They join you at birth, and help you move over into the spiritual realm when you part the earthly plane. They defend you when you're in trouble, guide you in the right direction according to your life plan, give you small insights into how things are, and inspire you to live better lives.

Today, you can share whatever feelings or hurt you are bearing in life with your Angel. Then know they will be there to help support you, guide you, and love you on your journey.

A DAY IN SPIRIT

December 19
Your Angels are helping you to connect with the Divine.

Your Angels have love and protection to impart, and, as such, their purpose is to provide you with a reflection of your true nature so that you may never really forget your connection with the Divine. Your Angels hold the blueprint of what you truly are so that you may awaken to your ultimate truth.

Today, while connecting with your higher power, know that your Angels are your guardians of hope and the keepers of your magic and your dreams.

December 20
Call on Archangel Chamuel for help.

His name means, "He who sees God." He inspires you to realize that you must first love yourself in order to love others. He gently guides you to view your own shortcomings. Chamuel helps you with world peace, your careers, lost items, and your life's purpose. He helps with relationships and can lift your spirit in the depths of sorrow to find love in your hearts.

Today, call on Archangel Chamuel to guide your thoughts and actions and to help bring good relationships into your life.

December 21
Call on Archangel Gabriel for help.

Her name means, "Strength of God" or "The Divine is my strength." Of the seven Archangels, Gabriel is the only Archangel portrayed as a woman. Gabriel carries and instills love, truth, joy, justice, and grants wisdom in interpreting dreams and visions. She can guide you with your life purpose in arts and communication.

Today, call on Archangel Gabriel for creative expression through writing or delivering healing messages.

December 22

Call on Archangel Jophiel for help.

This Angel inspires you toward awareness, enlightenment, open-mindedness, and freedom of thought. He teaches your consciousness to discover the light within. His name means, "Beauty of God" or "Divine Beauty." Jophiel is the patron of artists, helping with artistic projects, and thinking beautiful thoughts. Jophiel helps in fighting pollution, cleaning up our planet, and brings to mankind the gift of beauty.

Today, call on Archangel Jophiel for absorbing information, studying for and passing tests, dissolution of ignorance, pride, narrow-mindedness, and exposure of wrongdoing in governments and corporations.

December 23

Call on Archangel Raphael for help.

Raphael is the Archangel of healing. He is known for extreme healing energy, which he bestows on everyone. His name means, "Healing power of God," "Divine Healer," or "God who heals." In Hebrew, the word rapha means doctor or healer, and he is a powerful healer of all living forms, including humans and animals. Besides healing, he can grant you creativity, grace, joy, and love.

Today, call on Archangel Raphael for anything you need help healing with any living being.

December 24

Call on Archangel Uriel for help.

His name means, "Fire of God" or "Light of God." Uriel kindles and rekindles the spark within your heart that God created. He also rules over music and literature. Uriel helps you to embrace your own psychic and spiritual gifts. Uriel warned Noah of the impending flood and gives you prophetic information and warning in your life. Uriel also helps to heal you and the earth after earthquakes, floods, fires, tornadoes, or any other natural disasters.

Today, call on Archangel Uriel when you need help with ideas or intellectual guidance, especially creative insights to your life's purpose.

December 25

Call on Archangel Michael for help.

Michael is the most well-known Archangel who strengthens your spirits during difficult times or dangerous situations. His name means, "One who is like God," "Who is like God," or "Who is like the Divine." It is, however, meant to be a question: "Who is like the Lord?" Archangel Michael inspires truth, patience, and love. He is the one that leads your souls to heaven. He is the leader of the Archangels and is in charge of protection, strength, courage, and truth.

Call on Archangel Michael if you need help during any crisis or emergency. When called upon, he will be there to help, guide, support, and protect you.

December 26

Call on Archangel Raguel for help.

His name means, "Friend of God." He oversees all other Angels and Archangels. You can call on him for help when you need to be empowered and respected. Raguel helps resolve arguments and creates harmony for family and friends.

Call on Archangel Raguel to help resolve conflicts in relationships, solve stressful problems, and to help people who are neglected or oppressed.

December 27

At every moment you make a choice.

At every moment in your life you have a choice that will either lead you closer to your spirit or further away from it. Chose to let your bright spirit shine. Sometimes life can be difficult, but the more pain and suffering you have in your life, the more you can connect to humanity and the concept of oneness, the more you have a chance to heal and to help others heal through your own pain and suffering.

Today, make a choice to heal and evolve through your spirit no matter how easy or how hard your path. Through this, you will be able to connect and help others for this is a great gift.

A DAY IN SPIRIT

December 28

Seek knowledge and seek your truth.

Your knowledge that you seek is gained by the conscious reflection and integration of your experiences, observations, and thoughts. Your knowledge is defined by the expertise and skills you have acquired through your spiritual experiences and education, the spiritual understanding of your lessons, and the awareness gained by the knowledge and truth you seek in your life.

Today, see the world as it is — not as you are. Bless yourself today to have the knowledge and truth to help you gain wisdom on your spiritual journey.

December 29

Gather your wisdom as you grow.

The wisdom you acquire transcends time during your cycles of reincarnation and karma. It applies to all your past, present, and future lives. Wisdom is the understanding of divine principles, of the relationship between yourself, others, and the earth. It is a mixture of knowledge tempered with love, or love tempered with knowledge because with knowledge or conscious reflection of your circumstances, you can always accept your lessons and learn from them.

Today, gather wisdom and a deeper understanding and spiritual realization of people, things, events, or situations that will result in the ability to choose or act on a greater spiritual level.

December 30

Have faith, hope, and love.

Faith is the confident belief or trust in a person, idea or concept that is not based on proof. Hope is the belief in a positive outcome related to events and circumstances in your life. Love is the vibration of your infinite truth. It resonates within all spiritual beings. With balance of faith, hope, and love in your life, life can become effortless at best and challenging at worst, but never a struggle.

Today, have faith, hope, and love in your heart. These are amazing and incredible words. These words not only mean to wish for something but to wait with expectation for its fulfillment.

December 31

Live your light every day of your life.

As aware and conscious spiritual beings, it is important to hold the light not only on yourself but also on those who can't, won't, or don't know how to hold the light on themselves. You made an agreement before you were born as to what your purpose is and how you are going to live your life to achieve that purpose and help humanity. Shine your light every day on all who cross your path like the brave and wise soul that you are.

Today, see the light that you hold within yourself. Be and live the beautiful light that you are.

CPSIA information can be obtained
at www.ICGtesting.com
Printed in the USA
FSOW03n1132150917
38524FS